COMPACT *Research*

HPV

Diseases and Disorders

ReferencePoint Press®

San Diego, CA

Other books in the Compact Research Title Category set:

Acne and Skin Disorders
Bipolar Disorder
Brain Tumors
Breast Cancer
Concussions
Hepatitis
Herpes
Influenza
Sexually Transmitted Diseases

*For a complete list of titles please visit www.referencepointpress.com.

COMPACT *Research*

HPV

Peggy J. Parks

Diseases and Disorders

ReferencePoint
Press®

San Diego, CA

© 2015 ReferencePoint Press, Inc.
Printed in the United States

For more information, contact:
ReferencePoint Press, Inc.
PO Box 27779
San Diego, CA 92198
www.ReferencePointPress.com

Picture credits:
Accurate Art, Inc: 32–33, 45–47, 59–61, 73–75
© John Amis/AP/Corbis: 18
Steve Gschmeissner/Carol Upton/Science Photo Library: 12

LIBRARY OF CONGRESS CATALOGING-IN-PUBLICATION DATA

Parks, Peggy J., 1951-
  HPV / by Peggy J. Parks.
    pages cm. -- (Compact research series)
  Audience: Grades 9 to 12.
  Includes bibliographical references and index.
  ISBN 978-1-60152-690-8 (hardback : alk. paper) -- ISBN 1-60152-690-3 (hardback : alk. paper)
 1. Papillomavirus diseases--Juvenile literature. I. Title. II. Title: Human papillomavirus.
  RC168.P15P367   2015
  616.9'11--dc23
                                                                    2014007191

Contents

Foreword

"Where is the knowledge we have lost in information?"

—T.S. Eliot, "The Rock."

As modern civilization continues to evolve, its ability to create, store, distribute, and access information expands exponentially. The explosion of information from all media continues to increase at a phenomenal rate. By 2020 some experts predict the worldwide information base will double every seventy-three days. While access to diverse sources of information and perspectives is paramount to any democratic society, information alone cannot help people gain knowledge and understanding. Information must be organized and presented clearly and succinctly in order to be understood. The challenge in the digital age becomes not the creation of information, but how best to sort, organize, enhance, and present information.

ReferencePoint Press developed the *Compact Research* series with this challenge of the information age in mind. More than any other subject area today, researching current issues can yield vast, diverse, and unqualified information that can be intimidating and overwhelming for even the most advanced and motivated researcher. The *Compact Research* series offers a compact, relevant, intelligent, and conveniently organized collection of information covering a variety of current topics ranging from illegal immigration and deforestation to diseases such as anorexia and meningitis.

The series focuses on three types of information: objective single-author narratives, opinion-based primary source quotations, and facts and statistics. The clearly written objective narratives provide context and reliable background information. Primary source quotes are carefully selected and cited, exposing the reader to differing points of view, and facts and statistics sections aid the reader in evaluating perspectives. Presenting these key types of information creates a richer, more balanced learning experience.

For better understanding and convenience, the series enhances information by organizing it into narrower topics and adding design features that make it easy for a reader to identify desired content. For example, in *Compact Research: Illegal Immigration*, a chapter covering the economic impact of illegal immigration has an objective narrative explaining the various ways the economy is impacted, a balanced section of numerous primary source quotes on the topic, followed by facts and full-color illustrations to encourage evaluation of contrasting perspectives.

The ancient Roman philosopher Lucius Annaeus Seneca wrote, "It is quality rather than quantity that matters." More than just a collection of content, the *Compact Research* series is simply committed to creating, finding, organizing, and presenting the most relevant and appropriate amount of information on a current topic in a user-friendly style that invites, intrigues, and fosters understanding.

HPV
at a Glance

HPV Defined

Human papillomavirus (HPV) is a large family of viruses; thirty to forty of them can infect the genital area of males and females and are considered sexually transmitted diseases (STDs).

HPV Types

Scientists categorize HPVs into two groups: low risk (wart causing) and high risk (cancer causing).

HPV Infection

Unlike many other viruses, HPVs infect only skin cells; these may be cutaneous (visible) skin or the skin of the body's warm, moist, mucous membranes.

Genital HPV Prevalence

According to the Centers for Disease Control and Prevention (CDC), HPV is the most common of all STDs, with an estimated 79 million cases currently affecting males and females in the United States.

Transmission of HPV

Genital HPVs are spread most often through sexual intercourse, but may also be spread through oral sex or any type of skin-to-skin contact with infected genital areas.

Health Risks

High-risk HPVs are associated with numerous types of cancer, the most common of which is cervical cancer.

Symptoms of Infection

Certain HPV strains cause genital warts, so symptoms are obvious; high-risk strains often cause no symptoms and are discovered only when problems develop, such as the onset of cancer.

Factors That Increase Risk

Anyone who is sexually active is at risk for HPV infection, but risk is highest for those with multiple sex partners and those with impaired immune systems.

Diagnosis

Two tests, the Pap smear and HPV DNA test, are used to detect abnormal cells and/or HPV infection in women, but there is no test for men.

Treatment

HPV infection is incurable, but people can undergo treatments for many of the health problems associated with it.

Prevention

Preventing HPV infection is challenging, since even touching someone's genitals can spread it. Vaccinations can protect against HPVs that cause most cases of genital warts, cervical cancer, and several other types of cancers.

HPV Vaccine Controversy

Mandating HPV vaccination is an extremely controversial prospect; many states and territories have other types of HPV legislation in place, but only in Virginia and Washington, DC, is the vaccine mandatory.

Overview

In October 2012 a college student posted an article online about her struggle with a sexually transmitted virus known as HPV. She explains how her nightmare began the day her boyfriend called to tell her that he was infected. After discovering a small white bump on his penis, he had gone to a doctor, who confirmed that it was a genital wart—a symptom of HPV infection, which he had likely passed along to her. At first she was so taken aback by what he said that she thought he was playing a joke on her. "My boyfriend told me he (now we) had genital warts," she says. "I laughed for thirty seconds until I realized he wasn't joking." She became terribly distraught, and grew even more so when she, too, developed genital warts and had to have them surgically removed. "I felt dirty, infected, and terrified,"[1] she says.

Working Through the Angst

The woman was furious with her boyfriend for infecting her, and for weeks she could barely stand to look at him. Then she began to realize that he was also having a difficult time. "My boyfriend was a wreck," she says. "He felt ashamed, responsible, and incredibly guilty."[2] They decided to spend time researching HPV in order to learn as much as they could about it, and the first thing they discovered was that it was the most common of all STDs. Even on their own college campus, one out of every three students was assumed to be infected with the virus.

Hearing those statistics was somewhat comforting, but the woman still felt a great deal of shame. Eight or nine months passed before she could look at herself in the mirror without feeling disgusted, and even more time passed before she regained her self-esteem. "It took me two years to realize I wasn't dirty," she says. Through reading online discussions about HPV, talking openly with her boyfriend, and confiding in a few trusted friends, she finally stopped viewing herself in such a negative light. "Sexually transmitted infections should be treated just like other infections," she says, "with medical attention and care and not with judgement, stigma, and self-loathing."[3]

What Is HPV?

Although *human papillomavirus* sounds like a singular term, HPV is actually a large family of viruses. Scientists have discovered an estimated 180 HPV types, or strains, each of which has its own unique DNA structure. These strains are all identified by numbers and are loosely categorized into two groups: low-risk (wart-causing) types and high-risk (cancer-causing) types, based on whether they put someone at risk for cancer. "Low-risk HPV types can cause genital warts and low-grade changes in the cells, but rarely cause cancer," says the American Cancer Society. "High-risk HPV types can cause low-grade changes, high-grade changes, pre-cancer, and cancer."[4]

> " Although *human papillomavirus* sounds like a singular term, HPV is actually a large family of viruses. "

Most of the known HPV strains can cause papillomas (the scientific term for "warts"), which can grow on the skin of the hands, arms, chest, feet, and toes. Thirty to forty HPVs can infect the genital areas of males and females, as well as the lining of the mouth and throat.

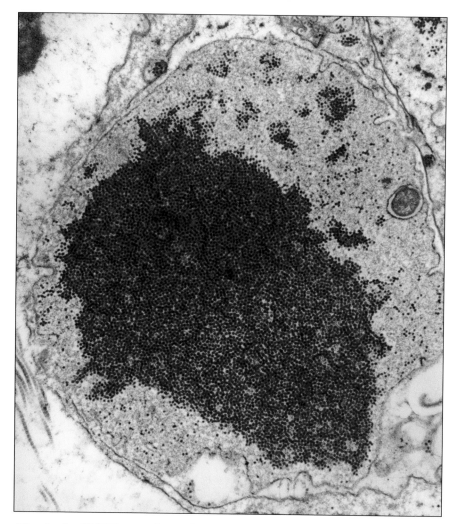

Hundreds of HPV particles (red) infect a host cell, as seen through a colored transmission electron micrograph. High-risk strains of the virus have been linked to cervical cancer.

Like all viruses, those in the HPV family are microscopic organisms that are not capable of reproducing on their own. Rather, they must seek out and invade living cells as hosts and then hijack the cells' reproductive machinery to make more viruses. One trait that distinguishes HPVs from other viruses is the kinds of cells they attack, as the American Cancer Society explains: "For example, cold and flu viruses find and invade cells that line the respiratory tract (nose, sinuses, breathing tubes, and lungs).

The human immunodeficiency virus (HIV) infects the T-cells and macrophages of the immune system. HPV infects *squamous epithelial cells.*"[5] Squamous epithelial cells are thin, flat cells that cover the skin's surface and are also found in mucous membranes. These are the warm, moist, skin-like layers that line the inside of the mouth, as well as the vagina, anus, cervix (base of the womb at the top of the vagina), vulva (around the outside of the vagina), head of the penis, mouth, throat, trachea (the main breathing tube), bronchi (smaller breathing tubes branching off the trachea), and lungs.

How HPV Is Spread

HPVs are highly contagious viruses. Common warts, for instance, easily spread when someone with breaks in the skin (even microscopic cuts) touches an object used by an infected person. This allows the virus to enter the person's body. Although people of all ages can contract and spread warts, they are especially common among children. A widely accepted theory is that children commonly suffer from scrapes, cuts, and hangnails. If they are exposed to HPV, these breaks in the skin provide an ideal way for the virus to enter their bodies.

Mucosal HPVs can spread in a number of ways, most commonly through vaginal or anal sex. They can also spread during oral sex, as well as through skin-to-skin contact—even without sexual intercourse, as the Throat Cancer Foundation writes: "The virus lives in the skin and spreads via skin to skin contact." The group says this differentiates HPVs from other STDs like chlamydia and HIV, both of which are spread through bodily fluids. "This means you can contract HPV through things like vaginal and anal sex, oral sex, mutual masturbation—anything where infected skin touches skin (it is important to remember your skin is not just on the outside). There just needs to be tiny microscopic cuts for HPV to be transferred from person to person."[6]

Prevalence of Genital HPV

HPV is the most common of all STDs, and it also accounts for the majority of newly acquired STDs. "Anyone who is having . . . sex can get HPV," says the CDC, adding that nearly all sexually active men and women contract the virus at some point in their lives. The agency goes on to say: "This is true even for people who only have sex with one person in their lifetime."[7] The World Health Organization estimates that HPV affects more than 630 million people worldwide. In the United States, out of more than 110 million STDs affecting men and women, HPV accounts for approximately 79 million—nearly 72 percent of the total.

CDC research has also shown that the majority of new HPV infections are among youth. Although males and females of any age can contract HPV, infections are growing in prevalence among adolescents and young adults aged fifteen to twenty-four. In a June 2012 paper, researchers from New York City write: "This phenomenon is often attributed to both an earlier age of initial sexual contact as well as an increase in the total number of sexual partners."[8]

What Are the Health Risks of HPV?

In most people who are infected with HPV, the immune system gets rid of the virus, as San Francisco physician Robin Wallace explains: "HPV is a tough virus, but our immune systems are usually tougher. Our bodies start fighting off the virus immediately."[9] Sometimes, however, the immune system cannot rid the body of HPV, which can lead to cell changes that develop into cancer. Nearly 100 percent of cervical cancer cases are caused by infection with certain high-risk HPV strains, and the disease is the third leading cause of cancer death among women worldwide. Each year more than 240,000 women worldwide die of cervical cancer, with most from developing countries where diagnostic tests are often not available. In the United States cervical cancer is the most common form of HPV-related cancer. It affects an estimated 19,000 women each year and results in nearly four thousand deaths.

> **[Genital HPV] can also spread during oral sex, as well as through skin-to-skin contact—even without sexual intercourse.**

High-risk HPV strains are also associated with other types of cancer. Among women, according to the CDC, HPV causes 2,800 cancers of the anus, 2,100 cancers of the vulva, and 500 cancers of the vagina each year. Among men, 600 penile cancers and 1,500 anal cancers are attributed to HPV infection each year. Another growing problem is HPV-related oral cancer, whose prevalence has been on the rise. The CDC reports that nearly 12,000 new cases of HPV-associated oral cancers are diagnosed each year in the United States, including 2,370 in women and 9,356 in men.

HPV Warning Signs

The majority of people with HPV never develop any symptoms, which means they have no way of knowing they are infected. Says Stefanie Gefroh-Ellison, a physician from Fargo, North Dakota: "Only about 20 percent of people who have it will ever know they have it."[10] When symptoms do develop it is undoubtedly because the person has contracted one of the HPV strains that causes warts. Genital warts, for instance, often appear within a few months after contact with an infected partner. They may range in size from small to large and appear as red or white bumps, tiny cauliflower-like clusters, or flat flesh-colored bumps that are barely visible. In women genital warts may grow on the lips of the vulva, around the clitoris, in and around the anus, and on the linings of the vagina, cervix, and rectum. In men genital warts tend to develop on the tip and shaft of the penis and on the scrotum, as well as in and around the anus.

> " The majority of people with HPV never develop any symptoms, which means they have no way of knowing they are infected.

Strains of HPV that do not cause warts are even less likely to cause symptoms, as Philadelphia, Pennsylvania, physician Marie Savard explains: "Occasionally, people may notice itching or skin changes, but more often HPV is a silent infection."[11] HPV may linger in the body for many years and remain undetected. Over time, however, if cells in infected areas become abnormal and then turn cancerous, warning signs of cancer could begin to appear. Depending on the type and severity (how aggressive the cancer is), these could include anything from severe pain to abnormal bleeding and/or the development of tumors.

Who Is at Risk for HPV Infection?

Although anyone who is sexually active can contract HPV, certain factors can markedly increase someone's risk. One of the main risk factors is being involved with multiple sex partners or having sex with someone who has had multiple sex partners. Pediatrician Margaret J. Meeker explains: "Every time a person has sex with someone, it is like having sex with every person your partner has ever been with. This is an astounding concept but it is true. Most young people do not think it can happen to them . . . it is not surprising that the number of infected youth is so high."[12]

> **Although anyone who is sexually active can contract HPV, certain factors can markedly increase someone's risk.**

Also at high risk of contracting HPV are people whose immune systems have been weakened or damaged by disease. This is true of those who are infected with HIV, which is the virus that causes AIDS. The World Health Organization writes: "HIV-infected individuals are at higher risk of HPV infection and are infected by a broader range of HPV types."[13] Over time HIV destroys the immune system by killing the white blood cells that are crucial for fighting infection and disease. The sufferer is left dangerously vulnerable to all kinds of infections, including high-risk strains of HPV.

Diagnosis of Genital HPV Infection

Although there is no routine laboratory test for genital warts, a health-care provider can often diagnose them by examining the genital area and looking closely at the skin. According to the CDC, the diagnosis can be confirmed with a biopsy, which is warranted in certain circumstances. For example, a doctor might order a biopsy if he or she is not certain that the patient has an HPV infection, the lesions do not respond to standard therapy, the infection worsens during therapy, or if the patient has a weak immune system.

Since most HPV infections result in no visible symptoms, abnormal cell changes in an infected woman's cervix are most often found during routine screening called a Pap test (or Pap smear). During this procedure a health-care provider scrapes a small number of cells from the cervix, which are then examined under a microscope to look for cell abnormalities or precancerous conditions.

A separate HPV DNA test, which is designed to detect thirteen [ ]
risk HPV types, may also be performed by the health-care provider. T[ ]
American Cancer Society writes: "Doctors can now test for the types of
HPV (high-risk or carcinogenic types) that are most likely to cause cervical cancer by looking for pieces of their DNA in cervical cells. The test
is done similarly to the Pap test in terms of how the sample is collected,
and it sometimes can even be done on the same sample."[14] Because HPV
DNA tests can detect abnormalities that may not show up on Pap tests,
the American Cancer Society recommends that women over age thirty
have both tests done.

At this time, there is no test that can diagnose HPV infection in men.
But because gay men have a significantly higher risk of HPV-associated
anal cancer, some doctors encourage them to undergo anal Pap tests. A
2012 WebMD article on HPV infection in men explains: "In an anal Pap
test, the doctor collects cells from the anus, and then has them checked
for abnormalities in a lab."[15]

Treatment Options

As with all viruses, HPV is incurable, although there are treatments for
many of the health problems that are associated with it. For people with
genital warts, for instance, a number of treatment options are available.
The patient may be given prescription acid-based solutions to apply at
home and/or undergo surgical removal of the warts in a doctor's office,
hospital, or outpatient clinic. One method is a type of surgery known as
fulguration, which involves directing
a laser beam at the lesions to vapor-
ize and destroy them. Another surgical option is cryotherapy, in which
the warts are frozen off with blasts of
super-cold liquid nitrogen.

Treatments for high-risk HPV
infection revolve around preventing
or treating cancer that is associated

> " At this time, there is no test that can diagnose HPV infection in men. "

with the virus. For instance, a woman who has abnormal (precancerous)
cells on her cervix may undergo laser surgery or cryotherapy to destroy
the abnormal cells. Another option, if a doctor feels it is warranted, is
excision, in which the abnormal area on the surface of the cervix is cut

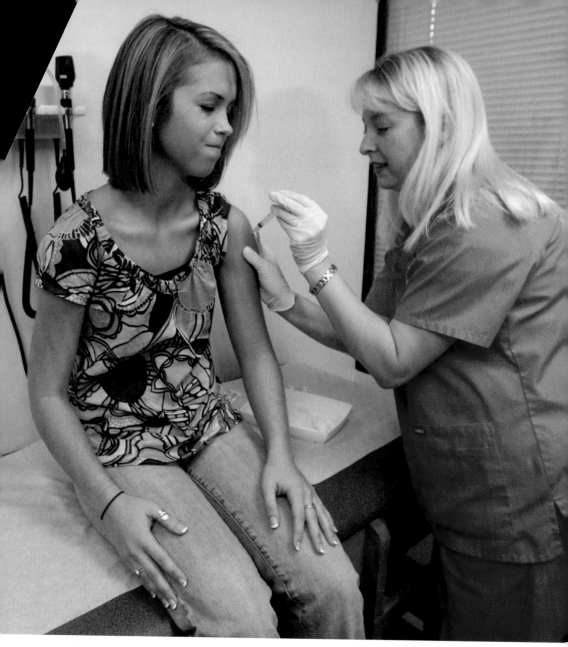

A young woman winces as she gets an HPV vaccine. Many medical and public health officials say that vaccination is the most effective way to prevent cervical cancer.

out. According to New York City physician Jason D. Wright, one benefit of excision is that it "helps to ensure that the abnormality is removed completely. If the edges of the tissue that is removed show evidence of the abnormality or precancer, further treatment may be needed."[16]

Can HPV Infection Be Prevented?

HPV is such a common STD and is so easily spread from person to person that the only sure way to avoid being infected is to refrain from any sort of sexual contact. "It's really pretty impossible to avoid acquiring one or more genital HPV infections if you decide you're going to be sexually active in your life," says Laura Koutsky, a professor and HPV expert at Seattle's University of Washington. "If we lock ourselves up in the house and don't associate with people, we won't get colds. If you never have sex, you won't get HPV. It's not clear we want to live that way."[17]

In the absence of swearing off sexual activity forever, there are steps people can take to reduce their risk of HPV infection. One important precaution is limiting the number of sex partners, as well as choosing partners who have done the same. Another precaution is using latex condoms, although they do not offer 100 percent protection against HPV. The National Cervical Cancer Coalition writes:

> Used correctly, condoms are very effective against STIs [sexually transmitted infections] such as gonorrhea and HIV that are spread through bodily fluids. However, they are likely to be less protective against STIs that spread through skin-to-skin contact, such as HPV and herpes. The reason is simply that condoms do not cover the entire genital area of either sex. They leave the vulva, anus, perineal area, base of the penis, and scrotum uncovered, and contact between these areas can transmit HPV.[18]

The group adds, however, that condoms should still be worn because consistent, correct use can lower the risk of acquiring HPV infection.

Should the HPV Vaccine Be Mandatory?

Health officials, as well as numerous physicians, stress that vaccination is the most effective way to prevent infection with the riskiest strains of HPV. Yet from the time that Gardasil, the first HPV vaccine, was introduced in June 2006, it has been embroiled in controversy. The issue became contentious soon after the vaccine's release, largely because health officials recommended that it be given to preteen girls. This remains a topic of debate today, with many parents unsure about what to do. But according to pediatrician Rodney Willoughby, there is a very good reason to vaccinate at a young age: protecting the child long before his or her first sexual encounter. "Ideally none of our children is going to be sexually active until they meet Mr. Right or Mr. Wrong, and that's the end of the story," says Willoughby. "But it happens, and sometimes you're not aware of it. And we can't prevent [HPV infection] once that exposure's occurred."[19]

> **In the absence of swearing off sexual activity forever, there are steps people can take to reduce their risk of HPV infection.**

For many people, even those who strongly support the HPV vaccine, the idea of the government mandating it is highly controversial. William Schaffner, who is chair of preventive medicine at Vanderbilt University School of Medicine, refers to the vaccine as "a wonderful advance in the prevention of cancer—for girls and women certainly, but also for boys and men."[20] Schaffner's objection is to the federal government exerting its power to make the vaccine mandatory. Rather, he believes it should be up to the people in each state to discuss and debate the issue and have the freedom to make their own decisions. "My prediction," says Schaffner, "is that, slowly, state by state, such mandates will be enacted because the vaccine is safe—and who does not wish to prevent as much cancer as they can?"[21]

A Public Health Problem

HPV is the most common of all STDs, and its prevalence continues to grow. Of more than 180 HPV strains that are known to exist, most cause no problems, and the majority of people who are infected do not even realize it. Some HPVs, however, are associated with health risks ranging from annoying warts to deadly types of cancer—which is why the vaccine debate has become so contentious in recent years. In coming years scientists will undoubtedly learn more about this family of viruses, and HPV may eventually not pose the threat that it does today. Until then, health officials consider it a formidable problem.

What Is HPV?

❝It can take weeks, months, or even years after exposure to HPV before symptoms develop or the virus is detected.❞

—The American Sexual Health Association, a source of reliable information on sexual health and STDs.

❝It is possible to have HPV and not know it, so a person can unknowingly spread HPV to another person.❞

—Immunization Action Coalition, a group that works to increase immunization rates and prevent disease by educating health professionals and the public.

As recently as the mid-1970s, scientists throughout the world assumed that HPV was one single virus. Its association with warts was well known, as this had been demonstrated in the early 1930s by American physician Richard E. Shope. During experiments with cottontail rabbits, he isolated the papillomavirus and correctly determined that it was highly contagious. Shope's work was later hailed as some of the most significant in viral research, although forty years passed before the true nature of HPV was known. This came about because of research by German virologist Harald zur Hausen—but at first the scientific world was not at all receptive to what he had to say.

Denouncing an Accepted Theory

Since the beginning of his medical career in the early 1960s, Hausen had been interested in infectious diseases; specifically the probable link between certain viruses and cancer. While conducting experiments in his laboratory in Würzburg, Germany, Hausen became increasingly skeptical of the prevailing scientific belief that cervical cancer was caused by the herpes simplex virus. He was convinced that the real culprit was HPV, but he had learned through research that it could not be the same strain as the one associated with common warts. This was Hausen's first indication that HPV was not a single virus after all; rather, it was an entire family of viruses, although he had no way of knowing how many strains there were.

In 1974 Hausen was one of the presenters at a Key Biscayne, Florida, conference on cervical cancer. Shortly before it was his turn to speak, he listened to an American researcher claim that he had established a link between cervical cancer and the herpes virus—which Hausen knew could not be true. Afterward he stood up and gave his own presentation, in which he boldly stated that the previous speaker's hypothesis was incorrect. He discussed his own studies and concluded by saying that the focus of cervical cancer research should no longer be on the herpes simplex virus but on HPV. When he finished speaking, he faced a stunned, silent, and obviously displeased group of scientists. "My statements were not well received," he says, "and I felt as a lonely voice in that meeting."[22] For Hausen, this rejection was the lowest point in his professional life. Still he had no doubt that he was on the right path and would not be dissuaded from following it.

> **Of the estimated forty mucosal HPVs that are known to exist, sixteen are considered high-risk strains.**

Hausen and his colleagues continued to aggressively pursue HPV research. One of their discoveries, that a strain associated with genital warts (HPV 6) was different from those linked to cervical cancer, was not at all surprising. They isolated type 11 and then went on to isolate the high-risk types 16 and 18, which are now known to cause the majority of cervical cancer cases. At long last, Hausen's work was gaining credibility with the scientific world, as he later discussed in an interview: "Until about 1979 or 1980, we had difficulties with our work. Not difficulties in doing it, but having it accepted in general. But after 1980, things gradually changed and when we finally isolated 16 and 18, which was published in 1983 and 1984, I think that changed the scene completely."[23]

A Multitude of Strains

In the years since Hausen's groundbreaking findings became public, HPV research has continued, and additional strains have been discovered. According to Cambridge University scientist Margaret A. Stanley, who is an expert on papillomaviruses, researchers have identified more than 180 HPV strains. At least three-fourths of these are associated with common warts, which are small, benign bumps that typically grow on the chest, hands, feet, fingers, and toes. Plantar warts, for instance, grow on weight-bearing areas of the feet, such as the heels and soles, and sometimes grow in clusters known as mosaic warts.

Warts of a different kind are caused by mucosal HPVs. These strains infect only mucosal areas of the body, as the American Cancer Society writes: "'Mucosal' refers to the body's mucous membranes, or the moist surface layers that line organs and cavities of the body that open to the outside."[24] Some areas where genital warts may be found in females are inside the vagina or anus, outside the vagina or anus or on nearby skin, and on the cervix inside the body. In males genital warts may grow on the penis, scrotum, groin area, thighs, and/or inside or around the anus. According to the CDC, HPV types 6 and 11 together cause 90 percent of all genital warts. The same mucosal HPV strains that cause genital warts can also cause warts on the lips, mouth, tongue, and in the throat, and the CDC refers to these as oral HPVs.

> **Although it is true that sexually active young people have a markedly higher risk of contracting HPV than those who are abstinent, refraining from sexual intercourse does not guarantee that someone is completely safe.**

Of the estimated forty mucosal HPVs that are known to exist, sixteen are considered high-risk strains. The most prevalent of these is type 16, followed by HPV 18 and 39. "That doesn't mean other strains cannot cause problems," says the Throat Cancer Foundation, "but these particular strains are known to be the biggest trouble makers."[25] The remaining mucosal strains that make up the high-risk group are HPV 31, 33, 35, 45, 51, 52, 56, 58, 59, 68, 69, 73, and 82. Because HPV research is widespread and ongoing, that list will undoubtedly expand as new strains are discovered.

The "Common Cold" of STDs

As the United States' leading health protection agency, the CDC is responsible for keeping track of all diseases and disorders that affect Americans and monitoring trends over time. This, of course, includes STDs, which the CDC watches closely because they are a serious problem. A February 2013 document prepared by the CDC revealed that as of 2008, there were more than 110 million STD cases nationwide. Nearly three-fourths of those cases were HPV, which makes it clear that HPV is the most prevalent STD in the United States. "Being told you have it is no big deal," says San Francisco physician Robin Wallace. "It's the common cold of the sexually active world."[26]

Beyond the CDC, scientists throughout the world perform their own studies on HPV. One that focused on evaluating the virus's prevalence was conducted between January 2008 and July 2011 by researchers from Athens, Greece, and involved 149 sexually active teenage girls. The team found that 62 of the girls tested positive for HPV. Of those, 30 were infected by multiple HPV types, and 54 had at least one high-risk strain. The most commonly identified HPV strain was the low-risk type 42, followed by high-risk types 51 and 59. In the published report, which appeared in the August 2012 issue of the medical journal *Gynecologic Oncology*, the authors write: "HPV infection rate was high in our sample. Furthermore a high percentage was infected with high risk types." They go on to say that "as age of first sexual intercourse drops,"[27] prevention strategies such as sex education and HPV vaccination become even more important to protect the health of young women and help stop the spread of HPV.

> " At the dawn of the twenty-first century, overall awareness of HPV was low to nonexistent. "

Sex Not Required

Although it is true that sexually active young people have a markedly higher risk of contracting HPV than those who are abstinent, refraining from sexual intercourse does not guarantee that someone is completely safe. This was revealed during a study by Cincinnati Children's Hospital pediatrician Lea E. Widdice and her colleagues. The study, which took place between 2008 and 2010, involved 259 females aged thirteen to twenty-one, of whom 190 were sexually experienced. Although the team found that those girls had the highest rates of HPV infection, 11.6 percent of the girls who had never had sexual intercourse also tested positive for at least one HPV strain. The final report of the study, which was published in August 2012, states that in the absence of sexual intercourse, the girls likely caught HPV through genital-to-genital or hand-to-genital contact. The authors write: "This demonstrates that sexually inexperienced females are at risk for HPV infection."[28]

A similar outcome resulted from a two-year study conducted in Rio de Janeiro, Brazil. Because the country has a severe problem with STDs, especially among young people, researchers wanted to examine the prevalence of HPV among adolescent girls. A total of one hundred females participated in the study, including fifty who were sexually active and ranged in age from thirteen to twenty, and another fifty who were virgins and ranged in age from eleven to twenty. Each of the girls underwent a gynecological exam during which vaginal swabs were taken for testing. Among the sexually active group, 66 percent tested positive for HPV, with 42 percent of those infected with high-risk strains. Of the second group, 6 percent tested positive for HPV despite the fact that they had never had sexual intercourse.

In the June 2013 published report, the study authors explain their findings about the Brazilian girls who were infected even though they

> " More than forty years have passed since Harald zur Hausen shocked and angered his fellow scientists by rebutting an accepted theory about cervical cancer. "

were virgins. The authors make it clear, however, that those who are sexually active have the highest risk. "It seems that the intercourse . . . is an important facilitating factor in the transmission of HPV, even though it is not required."[29] The report concludes with the study authors recommending that further research be pursued.

Awareness Still Lagging

At the dawn of the twenty-first century, overall awareness of HPV was low to nonexistent. Research consistently indicated this, including one study that was conducted during 2002 in the United Kingdom. It involved four hundred female university employees who agreed to answer a number of questions about HPV. When asked if they had ever heard of HPV infection, 70 percent said they had not. Of the 30 percent who had heard of HPV, most admitted that their knowledge of the virus was either vague or inaccurate. At the time the study was conducted, scientists and health officials worldwide were becoming aware of the high—and growing—prevalence of HPV. The 2002 report stated that HPV was among the most common causes of sexually transmitted infections, so discovering that women had such limited knowledge and awareness was a serious concern.

More than a dozen years have passed since that HPV study was conducted, and awareness has grown since then. Still, health officials and advocacy groups say that an alarming number of people do not understand what HPV is, how easily it can spread, and what problems it can cause. "Public awareness of the virus is extremely low," says the National Cervical Cancer Coalition. "Most people who contact us with questions about HPV have never even heard of HPV until they were diagnosed."[30]

A 2013 study to evaluate the level of HPV awareness was conducted by a team of researchers from Texas State University. A total of 411 college freshmen, about three-fourths of whom were female, participated in the study. When asked questions about their knowledge of HPV, only 38.8 percent knew that it was the most common of all STDs, and just 15 percent were aware that condoms did not fully protect against HPV infection. Fewer than 14 percent of participants were aware that HPV usually subsided without causing any health problems. In a May–June 2013 paper about the study, the team expressed its concerns about the findings: "Student knowledge of HPV has increased since the introduction of the

HPV vaccine and related media coverage, although knowledge on the subject is still low and often inaccurate."[31] The researchers say that because college-age students have a high risk of contracting HPV, educational efforts designed to help increase awareness and knowledge are crucial.

Progress and Challenges

More than forty years have passed since Harald zur Hausen shocked and angered his fellow scientists by rebutting an accepted theory about cervical cancer. He was confident in his knowledge, however, and refused to be discouraged from pursuing research that eventually came to be known as brilliant. Much has happened since that time, including the discovery of multiple HPV types, the specific parts of the body they infect, and their effects on people who contract them. As scientists continue their studies, additional HPV types will undoubtedly be discovered and more will be learned about the problems they can cause. As this is happening, public awareness of HPV will likely grow as well.

Primary Source Quotes*

What Is HPV?

> **"All types of HPV are spread by contact (touch). More than 40 types of HPV can be passed on through sexual contact, and are very common in sexually active people."**

—American Cancer Society, "Viruses," *Infectious Agents and Cancer*, March 7, 2013. www.cancer.org.

The American Cancer Society is a nationwide, community-based voluntary health organization that is dedicated to eliminating cancer as a major health problem.

> **"HPV is not the same as herpes or HIV (the virus that causes AIDS). Both viruses can be passed on during sex, but they have different symptoms and cause different health problems."**

—CDC, "Genital HPV Infection—Fact Sheet," July 25, 2013. www.cdc.gov.

The CDC is the United States' leading health protection agency.

* Editor's Note: While the definition of a primary source can be narrowly or broadly defined, for the purposes of Compact Research, a primary source consists of: 1) results of original research presented by an organization or researcher; 2) eyewitness accounts of events, personal experience, or work experience; 3) first-person editorials offering pundits' opinions; 4) government officials presenting political plans and/or policies; 5) representatives of organizations presenting testimony or policy.

❝HPV knowledge remains lowest among women who may be at highest risk for cervical cancer.❞

—Allison Friedman, Charles Ebel, and Raymond Maw, "Counseling the Patient with Genital HPV Infection," in *Sexually Transmitted Infections: Diagnosis, Management, and Treatment*, eds. Jonathan M. Zenilman and Mohsen Shawmanesh. Sudbury, MA: Jones & Bartlett, 2012, p. 301.

Friedman is a health community specialist with the CDC, Ebel is a researcher from North Carolina, and Maw is a physician from Belfast, Northern Ireland.

❝HPV is not exclusively a sexually transmitted disease.❞

—Stina Syrjänen, "Sexually Transmitted HPV Infections of the Oral Mucosa and Upper Respiratory Tract in Adults and Children," in *Sexually Transmitted Infections and Sexually Transmitted Diseases*, eds. Gerd Gross and Stephen K. Tyring. Berlin: Springer, 2011, p. 533.

Syrjänen is professor and head of the Department of Oral Pathology, Institute of Dentistry, at Finland's University of Turku.

❝Sexual contact with an infected partner, regardless of the sex of the partner, is the most common way the virus is spread.❞

—American College of Obstetricians and Gynecologists, "Human Papillomavirus Infection," February 2013. www.acog.org.

Composed of approximately fifty-five thousand physician members, the American College of Obstetricians and Gynecologists is the United States' leading advocate for women's quality health care.

❝I did not think I was susceptible to contracting a sexually transmitted disease because I am a lesbian. I did not realize that HPV could be transmitted from woman to woman contact.❞

—Sherry Tackett, foreword to *Your Cervix Just Has a Cold: The Truth About Abnormal Pap Smears and HPV*, by Brandie Gowie. New York: Morgan James, 2014, p. xi.

Tackett is a holistic nurse practitioner who specializes in women's health.

❝Although HPVs are usually transmitted sexually, doctors cannot say for certain when infection occurred.❞

—National Cancer Institute, "Human Papillomavirus (HPV) Vaccines," December 29, 2011. www.cancer.gov.

The National Cancer Institute is the federal government's principal agency for cancer research and training.

....

❝Much remains unknown about HPV transmission when symptoms (lesions such as warts or cell changes) aren't present.❞

—National Cervical Cancer Coalition, "HPV and Relationships," 2013. www.nccc-online.org.

The National Cervical Cancer Coalition is dedicated to serving women who have, or are at risk for, cervical cancer and other types of HPV-related disease.

....

Facts and Illustrations

What Is HPV?

- A June 2013 report by the Kaiser Family Foundation states that there are more than **6 million** new HPV infections annually in the United States.

- The CDC reports that about **14 million** people become newly infected with HPV each year.

- According to physician Melissa Conrad Stöppler, the majority of genital warts are caused by **HPV type 6** and **HPV type 11**, both of which are known as low-risk HPV strains.

- Philadelphia, Pennsylvania, physician Marie Savard says that researchers do not know whether people infected with HPV who have no symptoms are as **contagious** as those who do have symptoms.

- According to the National Cervical Cancer Coalition, when an HPV infection goes away, the immune system **"remembers"** that particular type and will prevent a new infection by the same type from occurring again.

- The American Sexual Health Association states that at any given time approximately **70 million** Americans are infected with HPV.

- The CDC says that there is not an approved HPV test to detect the virus in the **mouth or throat**.

HPV Is the Most Common STD

According to a February 2013 publication by the Centers for Disease Control and Prevention, more than 110 million STDs were reported among American men and women during 2008. As this graph shows, HPV was more than three times as prevalent as herpes simplex (HSV-2), and more common than any other type of STD.

Estimated Number of Sexually Transmitted Infections in the United States, 2008

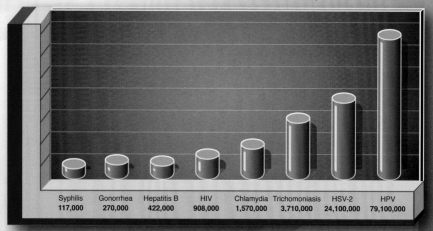

Syphilis	Gonorrhea	Hepatitis B	HIV	Chlamydia	Trichomoniasis	HSV-2	HPV
117,000	270,000	422,000	908,000	1,570,000	3,710,000	24,100,000	79,100,000

Source: Centers for Disease Control and Prevention, "Incidence, Prevalence, and Cost of Sexually Transmitted Infections in the United States," *CDC Fact Sheet,* February 2013.

- According to German scientist Andreas Kaufmann, **humans** are the only species affected by HPV.

- The National Cervical Cancer Coalition reports that among Americans aged fifteen to forty-nine, only **one in four** has not had a genital HPV infection.

- According to the CDC, of individuals who are infected with mucosal HPV, up to **30 percent** are infected with multiple types of the virus.

Awareness of HPV Is Still Lagging

Despite widespread publicity about HPV and HPV vaccines, many young women still lack awareness and knowledge of the virus. Examining this lack of awareness was the focus of a study by Florida State University researchers, who surveyed 739 women aged eighteen to twenty-six. As shown here, the participants had low to moderate knowledge of HPV.

Participants Giving Correct or "I don't know" Responses to HPV-Related Statements

Knowledge Determination Statements (T or F indicates correct response)	Correct response (%)	"Don't know" response (%)
HPV can cause genital herpes. (F)	25%	53%
Having one type of HPV means that you cannot acquire new types. (F)	55%	42%
Genital HPV infection can cause ovarian cancer in women. (F)	9%	31%
An abnormal Pap smear may indicate that a woman has HPV. (T)	66%	32%
Most genital HPV infections do not clear up on their own. (F)	16%	45%
Most women with genital HPV have visible signs or symptoms. (F)	66%	31%
HPV is the least common sexually transmitted infection in the US (F)	60%	38%
Genital warts are caused by HPV infection. (T)	30%	58%
Genital HPV infection can cause cervical cancer in women. (T)	84%	15%
A Pap test (Pap smear) is used to find precancerous cells on the cervix. (T)	79%	20%

Source: Mary E. Gerend and Janet E. Shepherd, "Correlates of HPV Knowledge in the Era of HPV Vaccination: A Study of Unvaccinated Young Adult Women," *Women & Health*, January 2011. www.ncbi.nlm.nih.gov.

- McGill University's division of Cancer Epidemiology in Montreal, Canada, reports that most HPV infections in young men and women last no more than **one or two years**.

- According to physician Melissa Conrad Stöppler, HPV is not found in blood or organs **harvested for transplantation**.

What Are the Health Risks of HPV?

> **"In cases where the virus cannot be fought off naturally, the body is at risk for serious complications, including cancer."**
>
> —Immunization Action Coalition, which works to increase immunization rates and prevent disease by educating health professionals and the public.

> **"Some types of HPV are simply more aggressive than others."**
>
> —Mary M. Gallenberg, an obstetrician/gynecologist with the Mayo Clinic in Rochester, Minnesota.

David Hastings owns a popular Cuban restaurant in Gulfport, Florida, and he also volunteers as a patient advocate with the Oral Cancer Foundation. He first became aware of the organization in 2006 when a doctor gave him the worst news of his life: He had oral cancer, and his prognosis was bleak. Hastings was shocked and frightened—and to make matters worse, no one could answer his questions. Even after seeing five different doctors, not one of them could explain how a healthy, fitness-conscious man who had never smoked and rarely drank alcohol could end up with cancer of the throat.

As time went by, Hastings grew even more frustrated, asking the same question over and over again: "If something is trying to kill you, don't you want to find out what it is?"[32] Finally, after months of agonizing over the unknown, he learned the cause of his cancer. Without knowing it, he was infected with a high-risk virus called HPV.

Spreading the Word

Hastings underwent an aggressive series of chemotherapy and radiation treatments that lasted seven weeks. He suffered from constant nausea, and his throat felt like it was on fire from the powerful radiation. He describes the whole experience as "brutal" and goes on to say: "You can't taste, make saliva or swallow. You're on high doses of painkillers, you can't work. I'm a very fit guy and I lost 30 percent of my body weight. There's no way around it."[33]

Hastings survived the grueling treatment regimen, but it took another two years of recuperation before he felt like himself again. Today he is cancer-free and active with the Oral Cancer Foundation, working to expand awareness of HPV and educate people about the risks involved with infection. He focuses mostly on men because he has learned that their awareness is especially low, and they, like him, may have caught the virus years ago without realizing it. Also, Hastings has observed that men typically have erroneous perceptions about what causes oral cancer. "My cancer was not caused by tobacco or alcohol," he says. "It was caused by a virus. Men need to pay attention."[34]

"Irrefutable Evidence"

HPV-related oral cancer typically originates in the oropharynx, which is the part of the throat at the back of the oral cavity (mouth). "It begins where the oral cavity stops," says the American Cancer Society. "It includes the base of the tongue (the back third of the tongue), the soft palate (the back part of the roof of the mouth), the tonsils, and the side and back wall of the throat."[35] The scientific name is oropharyngeal cancer, although it is commonly shortened to oral cancer.

One of the first scientists to extensively study HPV-related oral cancer is Maura Gillison, who is now one of the world's top experts on the subject. During the mid-1990s Gillison had just finished her medical residency and was working as an oncologist (cancer specialist) at the Johns Hopkins Oncology Center in Baltimore, Maryland. While conducting research on oropharyngeal cancer, she was startled to see evidence of a type that she had never seen before. Unlike the old, familiar oral cancer, which predictably resulted from smoking and heavy alcohol use, this new type was connected with HPV infection—and it was affecting people with no history of smoking or drinking. In 1998, when Gillison first mentioned the concept to the director of the cancer center where she worked, he just stared at her and said nothing. "That was the first clue that what I was doing was interesting to others," she says, "and had potential significance."[36]

> **HPV-related oral cancer typically originates in the oropharynx, which is the part of the throat at the back of the oral cavity (mouth).**

As intriguing as the discovery was, however, Gillison knew that proving the link would be fraught with challenges. Although it was widely known that HPV caused cervical cancer and some genital cancers, any connection it might have with oral cancer was uncharted territory. She embarked on a population study that involved comparing medical records of cancer patients with those of healthy individuals, and she meticulously documented the findings. This study continued for seven years. In 2005, when Gillison finally analyzed the data, she was stunned—people with head and neck cancers were fifteen times more likely to have HPV infection in their mouths or throats than those who were cancer free. This confirmed her previous research, and she was so excited she leaped out of her chair and began jumping around the laboratory. "The association was so incredibly strong," says Gillison, "it made me realize this was absolutely irrefutable evidence."[37]

A Disturbing Trend

In the years since Gillison made her initial discoveries, she has continued to be a leader in HPV-associated oral cancer research. She was able to differentiate between what she calls "two completely different diseases": the HPV-positive type, in which patients have had many oral sex partners but no history of smoking or heavy drinking; and HPV-negative oral cancer, in which patients have a history of heavy smoking and drinking but not of oral sex. Says Gillison: "They might superficially look similar—a patient comes in with a neck mass and their throat hurts—but

I realized what drove the pathogenesis [the diseases' development] was completely different in the two cases."[38]

Today HPV-positive oral cancer is viewed by health officials as an alarming problem. In the United States the CDC reports that nearly twelve thousand new cases are diagnosed each year, and the number is growing. "In the U.S., there is an active shift going on," says Gillison. "Fortunately thanks to tobacco policy and public-health awareness, the incidence rate for the classical head and neck cancer caused by smoking is declining. But unfortunately, the rate of oropharynx cancer is still going up and it's because of the HPV component."[39] Gillison took part in a 2011 study by scientist Anil K. Chaturvedi and other researchers. They found that incidence of HPV-positive oral cancers had increased by 225 percent from 1988 to 2004. If this trend continues, says Chaturvedi, HPV-positive oral cancers will surpass the number of cervical cancers by the year 2020.

> " No matter what type of cancer develops, the process starts with changes to cells. "

This disease is a growing concern to health officials not only in the United States but also in many other areas of the world. A study published in November 2013, which was also led by Chaturvedi, investigated cases of HPV-positive oral cancer in twenty-three countries across four continents. The team found that prevalence had grown significantly between 1983 and 2002, especially in developed countries and predominantly among men. In Europe, according to British cancer expert Hisham Mehanna, HPV-positive oropharyngeal cancers have nearly quadrupled in the past ten to fifteen years, and he has grave concerns about the future. "Our projection suggests that it's going to continue to increase significantly,"[40] he says.

When Cells Become Abnormal

No matter what type of cancer develops, the process starts with changes to cells. Trillions of cells make up the human body, and under normal circumstances they grow, divide to make new cells, and die in an orderly fashion. Sometimes, though, cells become damaged and lose the ability to control their growth, so they start growing out of control. When this happens to cells on a woman's cervix it can lead to dysplasia, which is not cancer but is considered a precancerous condition. Mayo Clinic physician Mary M. Gallenberg explains: "The term indicates that abnormal cells were found on the surface of the cervix. Cervical dysplasia can range from mild to severe, depending on the appearance of the abnormal cells. Dysplasia could go away on its own or, rarely, it could develop into cancer."[41]

> "Another type of cancer that is caused by HPV is anal cancer, and this association has been known for more than twenty-five years."

When Kate-Madonna Hindes was undergoing a routine gynecological exam in 2011, the last thing she expected to hear from the doctor was, "Your entire cervix is covered with dysplasia."[42] Hindes was shocked, because she had no idea anything was wrong. She was always diligent about having regular pelvic exams and Pap smears. She remembered that a few of her tests had come back abnormal, but her previous gynecologist said it was nothing to be concerned about—and she did not question him. Now Hindes was hearing something very different, and it was disturbing. During her exam the doctor explained that a healthy cervix was pink, whereas hers was white. "Instead of a beautiful and healthy cervix," she says, "mine was filled with potholes and eyesores."[43]

Hindes underwent numerous surgical procedures to remove the abnormal cells from her cervix. One method, known as loop electrosurgical excision, involves the use of a thin wire loop that performs like a scalpel. As the doctor holds the loop, an electrical current passes through it to cut away a thin layer of the cervix. This method usually has a 90 percent cure rate, but it was not effective at removing all cancerous tissue from Hindes's cervix. The same was true of additional treatments, so her doctors said her only option was to have a complete hysterectomy. She had the operation in May 2013 and remains hopeful that she has finally put the cervical cancer battle behind her.

Rising Prevalence

Another type of cancer that is caused by HPV is anal cancer, and this association has been known for more than twenty-five years. In 1988, for instance, a study by researchers from the United Kingdom found high-risk HPV type 16 in nearly 60 percent of the anal cancer samples they examined. HPV type 18 was also found, although in only a small number of samples. The team presented its findings during a June 1988 conference in Anaheim, California, and concluded with the following statement from the published report: "The results of this investigation closely parallel similar studies of cervical cancer and lend support to the concept of the involvement of HPV 16 and 18 in the development of anal and genital [cancers]."[44]

> " According to a 2013 study by researchers from Philadelphia, Pennsylvania, HPV may play a role in the development of lung cancer. "

Anal cancer is a fairly uncommon disease. According to the American Society of Colon & Rectal Surgeons, it accounts for an estimated 1 to 2 percent of all cancers that affect the intestinal tract. The prevalence is on the rise, however, as the group writes: "Unlike some cancers, the numbers of patients that develop anal cancer each year is slowly increasing."[45] The CDC adds that of the anal cancer cases that develop, an estimated 90 percent are caused by infection with high-risk strains of HPV.

Some groups have a much higher risk of developing anal cancer than others, such as sexually active gay and bisexual men. Their risk is about seventeen times higher than that of heterosexual men. This risk is even higher among gay men who are infected with HIV, as researcher Dorothy J. Wiley, who is an associate professor at the University of California–Los Angeles School of Nursing, explains: "Invasive anal cancer is a health crisis for gay, bisexual and other men who have sex with men. Right now, invasive anal cancer rates among HIV-infected men who have sex with men surpass rates for seven of the top 10 cancers in men."[46]

Emerging Theories

Since the 1970s, when Harald zur Hausen identified the link between cervical cancer and HPV, researchers have made innumerable discoveries. High-risk HPVs are now known to cause many types of cancer in men and women, including a variety of genital cancers, cancer of the anus, and oropharyngeal cancer, among others. Many scientists are convinced that research has only begun to reveal HPV-associated cancers and that more will be uncovered in coming years.

According to a 2013 study by researchers from Philadelphia, Pennsylvania, HPV may play a role in the development of lung cancer. The research team, led by oncologist Ranee Mehra, examined tissue samples from thirty-six nonsmokers who were diagnosed with the disease. About 6 percent of the samples showed signs of infection by high-risk HPV types 16 and 18. This finding was significant, says Mehra, because lung cancer kills more than 1 million people each year, and about 10 percent of those who develop the disease are nonsmokers. "Given how many patients develop lung cancer," she says, "if even a small percentage of those tumors stem from HPV, that ends up being a large number of patients." Although many questions remain, Mehra says that hopefully her study will fuel further research. "What we need," she says, "is a better understanding of why . . . cancer develops in some patients and not in others."[47]

Looking Ahead

Numerous health risks are associated with HPV, from oral cancer to cervical dysplasia, cervical cancer, and cancer of the anus. Scientists are also conducting studies to examine whether other types of cancer might also be related to high-risk strains of the virus. Although no one can predict the future, history has shown that the more researchers pursue theories and seek answers, the more likely they are to find what they seek. Thus, additional revelations about HPV and its health risks are likely to emerge in coming years.

What Are the Health Risks of HPV?

> ❝ HPV usually goes away on its own, without causing health problems. ❞

—CDC, "HPV and Men—Fact Sheet," *Sexually Transmitted Diseases (STDs)*, February 23, 2012. www.cdc.gov.

The CDC is the United States' leading health protection agency.

> ❝ HPV doesn't 'go away on its own,' it simply infects and then lays dormant. The virus never ultimately leaves your body once infected. ❞

—Kate-Madonna Hindes, "20 Million Mind-Blowing Statistics About HPV and Cancer," *Minnesota Blog Cabin*, *MinnPost*, June 26, 2012. www.minnpost.com.

Hindes, who underwent surgery for cervical precancer, is editor in chief of *Minnesota Business Magazine*.

Bracketed quotes indicate conflicting positions.

* Editor's Note: While the definition of a primary source can be narrowly or broadly defined, for the purposes of Compact Research, a primary source consists of: 1) results of original research presented by an organization or researcher; 2) eyewitness accounts of events, personal experience, or work experience; 3) first-person editorials offering pundits' opinions; 4) government officials presenting political plans and/or policies; 5) representatives of organizations presenting testimony or policy.

❝The medical risks of genital HPV do exist and should not be overlooked, but a key point is that for most people, HPV is a harmless infection that does not result in visible symptoms or health complications.❞

—National Cervical Cancer Coalition, "HPV and Relationships," 2013. www.nccc-online.org.

The National Cervical Cancer Coalition is dedicated to serving women who have or are at risk for cervical cancer and other types of HPV-related disease.

❝In many cases genital warts do not cause any symptoms, but they are sometimes associated with itching, burning, or tenderness.❞

—Melissa Conrad Stöppler, "Genital Warts (HPV) in Women," MedicineNet, 2013. www.medicinenet.com.

Stöppler is a physician who serves on the medical editorial board of MedicineNet and is chief medical editor of eMedicineHealth.

❝Only HPV infections that are persistent (do not go away over many years) can lead to cervical cancer.❞

—National Cancer Institute, "Human Papillomavirus (HPV) Vaccines," December 29, 2011. www.cancer.gov.

The National Cancer Institute is the federal government's principal agency for cancer research and training.

❝Women who test negative for the high-risk strains of HPV using the HPV test have almost no chance of developing serious cell changes in the near future. This can provide tremendous peace of mind.❞

—Marie Savard, "Human Papillomavirus, HPV," Healthy Women, April 4, 2013. www.healthywomen.org.

Savard is an internal medicine physician from Philadelphia, Pennsylvania, and a former ABC News medical contributor.

❝Pregnant women with HPV almost always have natural deliveries and healthy babies—it's very rare for a newborn to get HPV from the mother.❞

— American Sexual Health Association, "Ten Things to Know About HPV," 2013. www.ashapublications.org.

The American Sexual Health Association serves as a source of reliable information on sexual health and STDs.

❝There is a small chance that a pregnant woman with genital warts can pass HPV to her baby. In the rare case that this happens, the baby could develop warts in the throat or voice box.❞

—Allison Friedman, Charles Ebel, and Raymond Maw, "Counseling the Patient with Genital HPV Infection," in *Sexually Transmitted Infections: Diagnosis, Management, and Treatment*, eds. Jonathan M. Zenilman and Mohsen Shawmanesh. Sudbury, MA: Jones & Bartlett, 2012, p. 307.

Friedman is a health community specialist with the CDC, Ebel is a researcher from North Carolina, and Maw is a physician from Belfast, Northern Ireland.

What Are the Health Risks of HPV?

- A 2011 study published in the *Journal of Clinical Oncology* predicts that oral cancers caused by HPV will **surpass cervical cancers** in the United States by the year 2020.

- According to a June 2013 fact sheet by the Kaiser Family Foundation, men have a much lower risk than women for developing an HPV-related cancer and suffer from less than **25 percent** of reported cases.

- The American Cancer Society states that more than **20 percent** of cervical cancer cases are found in women over age sixty-five.

- The Oral Cancer Foundation reports that more than **90 percent** of men who have sex with men are infected with HPV in their anal canals.

- According to the National Cancer Institute, high-risk HPV infection accounts for approximately **5 percent** of all cancers worldwide.

- The group Cervical Cancer Action reports that HPV infection doubles the risk of acquiring **HIV**, the virus that causes AIDS, in women.

- According to Indiana University pediatrician Aaron E. Carroll, more than **250,000 women** worldwide die from cervical cancer each year.

A Global Killer

Cervical cancer, which is nearly always caused by high-risk strains of HPV, affects women throughout the world. As these tables show, the death rate is highest in Africa and lowest in the United States and other industrialized countries.

Countries with Highest Prevalence

Country	Annual Mortality Rate (per 100,000 women)
Zambia	38.6
Malawi	38.3
United Republic of Tanzania	37.5
Uganda	34.9
Mozambique	34.5
Zimbabwe	33.4
Mali	28.4
Ghana	27.6
Rwanda	25.4
Nigeria	22.9

Countries with Lowest Prevalence

Country	Annual Mortality Rate (per 100,000 women)
Norway	2.3
Israel	2.1
United Kingdom	2.0
Spain	1.9
France	1.8
Sweden	1.8
United States	1.7
Turkey	1.6
Italy	1.5
Australia	1.4

Source: Cervical Cancer-Free Coalition, "Cervical Cancer Global Crisis Card." May 2013. www.cervicalcancerfreecoalition.org.

HPV-Associated Cancers

HPV is widely known as the virus that causes cervical cancer. But as shown here, the virus can lead to many other types of cancer as well, including some that affect both men and women.

Cancers Associated with HPV – Women

Type	Annual cases
Cervical cancer	10,300
Anal cancer	2,800
Vulvar cancer	2,100
Oral cancer	1,700
Vaginal cancer	500

Cancers Associated with HPV – Men

Type	Annual cases
Oral cancer	6,700
Anal cancer	1,500
Penile cancer	600

Source: Centers for Disease Control and Prevention, " Genital HPV Infection – Fact Sheet," July 25, 2013. www.cdc.gov.

- Mayo Clinic physician Mary M. Gallenberg states that **smoking** increases the risk of cervical cancer among women infected with high-risk strains of HPV.

- The CDC reports that each year about **eight thousand men** in the United States are affected by HPV-associated cancers.

- According to physician Melissa Conrad Stöppler, some types of HPV (such as types 5 and 8) often cause **skin cancers** in people with a rare hereditary skin disorder known as **epidermodysplasia verruciformis**.

The Link Between Oral Sex and Cancer

People who contract high-risk types of HPV in their mouths have a higher risk of developing oral cancer than noninfected individuals, and oral sex is one of the main ways the virus is transmitted. A 2013 study conducted by researchers from Houston, Texas, found that the likelihood of HPV infection was related to the number of oral sex partners, as this graph shows.

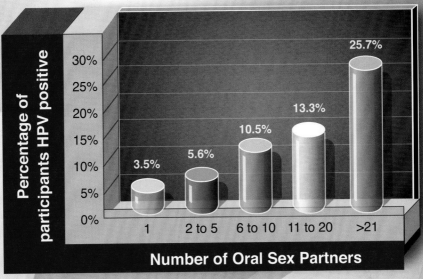

Source: Thanh Cong Bu et al., "Examining the Association Between Oral Health and Oral HPV Infection," *Cancer Prevention Research*, September 2013. www.ada.org.

- The National Cervical Cancer Coalition reports that HPV-associated cancers of the anus, penis, vagina, and vulva are rare in **industrialized countries**.

- According to physician Melissa Conrad Stöppler, in many developing countries cervical cancer is the most common type of cancer that is **fatal to women**.

Can HPV Infection Be Prevented?

Can HPV Infection Be Prevented?

66The only way never to get HPV is never to touch another human's genitals. Ever.99

—Aaron E. Carroll, a professor of pediatrics and assistant dean for research mentoring at Indiana University School of Medicine.

66For those who are sexually active, a long-term, mutually monogamous relationship with an uninfected partner is the strategy most likely to prevent HPV infection.99

—National Cancer Institute, the federal government's principal agency for cancer research and training.

In the early twentieth century, cervical cancer was the deadliest cancer for American women. "At that time," says world-renowned cancer expert Otis Webb Brawley, "it killed more women each year than breast or lung cancer."[48] The reason for such a bleak outcome was that cervical cancer was rarely caught at an early stage. There were no diagnostic tools that helped doctors find cell changes in a woman's cervix before the cells turned cancerous. As a result, the cancer progressed to an advanced stage before it was detected—and by then it was often too late to save the woman's life.

Today the situation is very different for women in the United States. When the American Cancer Society releases its ranking of the leading cancers among females, cervical cancer no longer appears in the top five or even in the top ten. What was once the most feared women's disease is now ranked fifteenth in terms of female cancer probability.

A Lifesaving Test

Cervical cancer prevalence started to decline in the mid-1950s after doctors began using a diagnostic procedure known as the Pap test. It is named after its creator, the late George N. Papanicolaou, a brilliant scientist who moved to the United States in 1913 from his native Greece. In the 1920s his research goal was to gain a better understanding of the human menstrual cycle, so he began studying vaginal cells under his microscope. Papanicolaou discovered that some of the cells he was peering at were abnormal, and those that were had come from a woman with cervical cancer. It was obvious to him that if cells found in vaginal fluid could be studied in this way, gynecological cancers could likely be detected at an early stage.

In 1928 at a conference in Battle Creek, Michigan, Papanicolaou presented a paper titled "New Cancer Diagnosis," in which he discussed his theory about cervical cancer. Members of the media were enthusiastic, and the *New York World* newspaper published a glowing article that stated: "Although Dr. Papanicolaou is not willing to predict how useful the new diagnostic method will be in the actual treatment of malignancy itself, it seems probable that it will prove valuable in determining cancer in the early stages of its growth when it can be most easily fought and treated."[49] To Papanicolaou's great disappointment, however, the response from his fellow scientists at the conference was nothing more than lukewarm. This was such a blow to him that he put the research on hold and spent the next decade focusing on other areas of scientific study.

> In the early twentieth century, cervical cancer was the deadliest cancer for American women.

Then in 1939, in collaboration with a fellow scientist named Herbert Traut, Papanicolaou returned to his cancer research. Within a few years the duo had published articles about their findings, and this led to greater awareness—as well as long-awaited acceptance by the medical community. By 1948 the American Cancer Society was officially endorsing the Pap test as a tool for the prevention of cervical cancer, and other medical groups did as well. Over the following years use of the test became more widespread. At the same time, the prevalence of cervical cancer plummeted in the United States. By the time of Papanicolaou's death in 1962, the total number of cases had declined by 70 percent, and they dropped even further over the following years. In an article about the scientist's life that was published in the journal *Lab Medicine*, the authors write: "Dr. Papanicolaou's legacy is the Pap test or Pap smear. . . . It is the most successful cancer screening test yet developed in the entire history of medicine."[50]

Benefits and Challenges of Inoculation

Another important tool for preventing HPV infection is vaccination, which is widely recommended by health officials and physicians. The US Food and Drug Administration (FDA) has approved two vaccines that are designed to prevent infection by four HPV strains. The first vaccine, known as Gardasil (or Silgard in Europe), was introduced in June 2006. It is known as a quadrivalent vaccine, with *quad* indicating that it protects against four HPV types: 6, 11, 16, and 18. In females Gardasil protects against cervical cancer and some cancers of the vulva, vagina, and anus that are known to be caused by HPV types 16 and 18. In males it can also protect against cancers associated with these strains of HPV, including anal, penile, and oral cancers. In both males and females the vaccine protects against genital warts caused by HPV types 6 and 11, which is about 90 percent of all genital warts.

> **Another important tool for preventing HPV infection is vaccination, which is widely recommended by health officials and physicians.**

The second vaccine, which was approved by the FDA in October 2009, is called Cervarix. It is approved only for females as an alternative to Gardasil and is a bivalent vaccine, meaning that it protects against two high-risk HPV strains: 16 and 18. Both Gardasil and Cervarix are given as a series of three shots over a six-month period.

As effective as these vaccines have proved to be, they do present some challenges. Neither can provide complete protection against every conceivable HPV-related disease. For instance, depending on which vaccine is chosen, protection is limited to HPV strains 16 and 18 or those two strains along with 6 and 11. The National Cancer Institute writes: "Overall, about 30 percent of cervical cancers will not be prevented by these vaccines. Also, in the case of Gardasil, 10 percent of genital warts will not be prevented by the vaccine. Neither vaccine prevents other sexually transmitted diseases, nor do they treat HPV infection or cervical cancer." The group emphasizes, however, that Gardasil and Cervarix are highly effective in preventing the HPV types that they are designed to target, and that being vaccinated is an essential part of HPV prevention: "Widespread vaccination has the potential to reduce cervical cancer deaths around the world by as much as two-thirds."[51]

One limitation of the HPV vaccines is that they are approved only for youth: males and females aged preteen through twenty-five or twenty-six—and no one older than that. This is because the vaccines work best when given to boys and girls long before they become sexually active. According to the research group the Kinsey Institute, in the United States the average age of first sexual intercourse is seventeen for both boys and girls, and an estimated 25 percent of teens become sexually active before age fifteen.

> "One limitation of the HPV vaccines is that they are approved only for youth: males and females aged preteen through twenty-five or twenty-six.

In addition, HPV vaccines are not effective if someone has already become infected—as a young woman named Bryce Covert was disturbed to learn. In January 2008, when Covert was twenty-four, she started seeing a young man with whom she became sexually involved. She had completed two out of three Gardasil vaccinations and had her third shot in March 2008. By June she had split up with her boyfriend. When Covert went to her gynecologist for a routine exam that month, she was shocked to learn that she had been infected with a high-risk strain of HPV. "On the phone, getting the news, I remember clearly that my first reaction was, 'But my boyfriend told me he didn't have any STDs,'" she says. "My doctor reminded me that men can't be detected as carriers—

and it's hard to pin down who gives it to you. My very next reaction was, 'But I've had the Gardasil vaccination.' To which she replied, 'Did you have intercourse before finishing your shots?' There was the problem."[52]

Benefits and Limitations of Condoms

Health officials stress that latex condoms, when used consistently and correctly, can vastly reduce the transmission of many STDs. But even though they can reduce the risk of HPV infection, condoms cannot provide complete protection from it. This is because the virus is spread not through bodily fluids such as semen or blood, but via skin-to-skin contact. Although a man's penis may be covered by the condom, skin in his or his partner's genital area that is not covered may be teeming with viruses.

Ricki Pollycove, who is an obstetrician/gynecologist in San Francisco, sees many cases of STDs in her medical practice. She says that people are often not aware that condoms cannot provide 100 percent protection against all HPV infections, and finding this out is often a shock. "Women diagnosed with HPV are often mystified and frustrated," she says, "having been 'super careful,' or picky, in choosing intimate partners and faithfully using condoms for all intercourse."[53] Pollycove cites studies by researchers at the University of California–San Francisco that have confirmed the ineffectiveness of condoms at protecting against HPV. These studies have found that viral particles of HPV can end up clinging to the outer surface of condoms. These particles may originate in areas of the man's scrotum or penile shaft that are not completely covered, or in the woman's vulva or vaginal tissue. Once the condom has viral particles on it, it becomes useless for protection against HPV infection.

> **With the prevalence of HPV-associated oral cancer on the rise, health officials are scrambling to find ways to slow or stop this alarming trend.**

Transmission of HPV often happens without the partners' knowledge because they have no symptoms—and therefore have no idea they are infected. "Passing a virus without having any symptoms is why these viruses get spread far and wide," says Pollycove. "Like bees sharing pollen flower to flower, men regularly transmit HPV . . . without knowing it." She acknowledges that women can also be symptom free and infect their partners with HPV, but there is a much greater likelihood that men will do so. Female-to-male infectivity is estimated at less than 5 percent of the rates of male-to-female transmission.

Brushing Teeth to Prevent Oral Cancer?

With the prevalence of HPV-associated oral cancer on the rise, health officials are scrambling to find ways to slow or stop this alarming trend. Researchers from the University of Texas Health Science Center in Houston were curious about whether poor oral health might contribute to incidence of cancer, so they conducted a study in 2013 to evaluate this. Noting previous research findings that cited risk factors such as oral sex, number of lifetime sex partners, and smoking, the report authors write:

> We found no previous study that examined the relationship between oral HPV infection and oral health. It is unclear whether poor oral health may increase the risk of oral HPV infection . . . or whether good oral health may compensate for the risk attributable to smoking or oral sex. Addressing these questions is important because these behavioral risk factors for oral oncogenic [cancer-causing] HPV infection are modifiable and preventable. Thus, this study's aims are two-fold: to examine the relationship between oral HPV infection and oral health, and to examine the interactive effect of oral health, smoking, and oral sex on oral HPV infection.[54]

The study involved more than thirty-four hundred men and women aged thirty to sixty-nine. Participants all provided data on their oral health and on their HPV-infection status before the study began. At its conclusion, the team discovered that poor oral health is an independent risk factor for oral HPV infection, irrespective of smoking status and/or oral sex behavior. Specifically, participants who reported poor oral health had a 56 percent higher rate of HPV infection than those whose mouths were healthy. People who reported having gum disease and dental problems had a 51 percent higher risk of being infected with HPV than those who did not. According to lead researcher Thanh Cong Bui, the study findings suggest that it may be fairly easy to control HPV in the throat by brushing teeth regularly and keeping the mouth environment clean. Says Bui: "The good news is, the risk factor is modifiable—by maintaining good oral hygiene and good oral health, one can prevent HPV infection and subsequent HPV-related cancers."[55]

No Simple Answers

In the years since George N. Papanicolaou created his famous Pap test, cervical cancer has changed from being the leading killer of women to a disease that can be detected and treated at an early stage. HPV infection, however, has not diminished over that time, and in fact, incidence has increased. That means consistent condom use, vaccinations, and other prevention strategies are more important than ever—although the proliferation of HPV makes prevention a challenging task. Perhaps the same brilliance and tenaciousness that allowed Papanicolaou to create a lifesaving test will also someday yield superior methods of prevention.

Can HPV Infection Be Prevented?

"It might be possible to prevent genital HPV infection by not allowing others to have contact with your anal or genital area, but even then there could be other ways to become infected that aren't yet clear."

—American Cancer Society, "Anal Cancer," January 2, 2013. www.cancer.org.

The American Cancer Society is a nationwide, community-based voluntary health organization that is dedicated to eliminating cancer as a major health problem.

....

"HPV is transmitted skin to skin, so protection by condoms is imperfect."

—Committee on Infectious Diseases, "HPV Vaccine Recommendations," *Pediatrics*, March 2012. http://pediatrics.aappublications.org.

The American Academy of Pediatrics' Committee on Infectious Diseases monitors and reports current developments in the prevention, diagnosis, and treatment of infectious diseases.

....

* Editor's Note: While the definition of a primary source can be narrowly or broadly defined, for the purposes of Compact Research, a primary source consists of: 1) results of original research presented by an organization or researcher; 2) eyewitness accounts of events, personal experience, or work experience; 3) first-person editorials offering pundits' opinions; 4) government officials presenting political plans and/or policies; 5) representatives of organizations presenting testimony or policy.

❝Genital warts can be very infectious to partners. Avoiding sex (including genital-to-genital contact) is the only sure way to prevent passing HPV to partners.❞

—Allison Friedman, Charles Ebel, and Raymond Maw, "Counseling the Patient with Genital HPV Infection," in *Sexually Transmitted Infections: Diagnosis, Management, and Treatment*, eds. Jonathan M. Zenilman and Mohsen Shawmanesh. Sudbury, MA: Jones & Bartlett, 2012, p. 306.

Friedman is a health community specialist with the CDC, Ebel is a researcher from North Carolina, and Maw is a physician from Belfast, Northern Ireland.

❝Be aware that spermicidal foams, creams or jellies are not effective against any sexually transmitted disease (STD), including HPV.❞

—Marie Savard, "Human Papillomavirus, HPV," Healthy Women, April 4, 2013. www.healthywomen.org.

Savard is an internal medicine physician from Philadelphia, Pennsylvania, and a former ABC News medical contributor.

❝It is not known how much condoms protect against HPV. Areas not covered by a condom can be exposed to the virus.❞

—FDA, "HPV (Human Papillomavirus)," December 9, 2013. www.fda.gov.

The FDA is responsible for protecting the public health by assuring the safety and effectiveness of America's food supply, human and veterinary drugs, and other products.

❝Female condoms cover more skin and may provide a little more protection than male condoms.❞

—American College of Obstetricians and Gynecologists, "Human Papillomavirus Infection," February 2013. www.acog.org.

Composed of approximately fifty-five thousand physician members, the American College of Obstetricians and Gynecologists is the United States' leading advocate for women's quality health care.

❝People can . . . lower their chances of getting HPV by being in a faithful relationship with one partner, limiting their number of sex partners, and choosing a partner who has had no or few prior sex partners.❞

—CDC, "Genital HPV Infection—Fact Sheet," July 25, 2013. www.cdc.gov.

The CDC is the United States' leading health protection agency.

❝Abstinence from sexual activity can prevent the spread of HPVs that are transmitted via sexual contact, but a person who abstains from sex may still become infected with other HPV types, such as those that cause common skin warts.❞

—Melissa Conrad Stöppler, "Genital Warts (HPV) in Women," MedicineNet, 2013. www.medicinenet.com.

Stöppler is a physician who serves on the medical editorial board of MedicineNet and is chief medical editor of eMedicineHealth.

Facts and Illustrations

Can HPV Infection Be Prevented?

- The National Cancer Institute reports that widespread HPV vaccination could potentially reduce cervical cancer deaths worldwide by as much as **two-thirds** if all women were vaccinated.

- According to the National Cancer Institute, after the Pap test became widely available in the 1950s, US cervical cancer incidence and death rates had declined more than **60 percent** by 1992.

- A survey published in December 2011 by researchers from Berlin, Germany, found that among women aged eighteen to twenty, the majority did not know that HPV is sexually transmitted, meaning they were not aware of steps needed to **prevent** infection.

- According to the National Cancer Institute, about **30 percent** of cervical cancers and 10 percent of genital warts are not preventable with HPV vaccines.

- The CDC says that to be most effective in helping prevent HPV infection, **condoms** should be used with every sex act, from start to finish.

- According to an October 2012 report on the status of cancer in the United States, **Mississippi** has an extremely low prevalence of Pap testing and some of the highest cervical cancer rates in the country.

Reducing the Risk

Health officials say that not having any sexual contact is the only sure way to avoid contracting HPV. But as shown here, there are steps that sexually active people can take to help lower their chances of becoming infected.

Latex condoms can help protect against contracting HPV; they are not 100 percent effective, however, because the virus can infect areas of skin that are not covered by the condom.

Being in a faithful relationship with one partner.

Limiting the number of sex partners and/or being with a partner who has had no or few prior sex partners.

Vaccinations can protect females against two high-risk HPV types that cause most cases of cervical cancer, as well as anal, vaginal, and vulvar cancers, and can protect males against anal and penile cancers. Vaccines can protect both males and females against most cases of genital warts.

Source: Centers for Disease Control and Prevention, "Prevention: How Can People Prevent HPV?," February 5, 2013. www.cdc.gov.

- According to the American Cancer Society, having **fewer sex partners** and avoiding sex with people who have had many other sex partners helps lower a person's risk of exposure to HPV.

- A survey published in December 2011 by researchers from Berlin, Germany, found that **51 percent** of female participants and **42 percent** of male participants thought that only women could be infected with HPV.

- According to the American Cancer Society, **50 percent** of women diagnosed with invasive cervical cancer have never had a Pap test, and another **10 percent** of those diagnosed had not had a Pap test in the five years prior to diagnosis.

Screening Lowers Cervical Cancer Risk

Prior to the 1950s cervical cancer was one of the deadliest types of cancer for American women. Today, largely because of screening techniques such as the Pap test and ways of treating abnormal cells before they become cancerous, cervical cancer prevalence has steadily declined in the United States. This is evident in the American Cancer Society's list of cancers that affect women, where cervical cancer is ranked fifteenth.

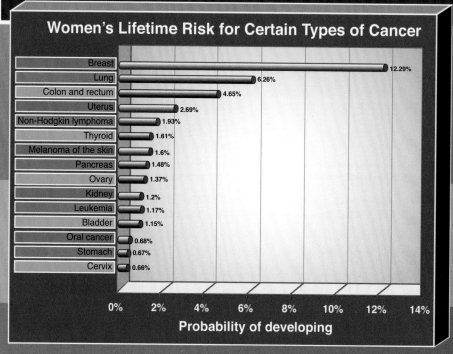

Women's Lifetime Risk for Certain Types of Cancer

Type	Probability of developing
Breast	12.29%
Lung	6.26%
Colon and rectum	4.65%
Uterus	2.69%
Non-Hodgkin lymphoma	1.93%
Thyroid	1.61%
Melanoma of the skin	1.6%
Pancreas	1.48%
Ovary	1.37%
Kidney	1.2%
Leukemia	1.17%
Bladder	1.15%
Oral cancer	0.68%
Stomach	0.67%
Cervix	0.66%

Source: American Cancer Society, "Lifetime Risk of Developing or Dying from Cancer," September 5, 2013. www.cancer.org.

- The National Cancer Institute states that although condoms are not foolproof, research has shown that correct, consistent condom use can **reduce the transmission** of HPV between sexual partners.

- According to the CDC, women can lower their risk of cervical cancer by getting **routine screenings** from ages twenty-one to sixty-five and following up on any abnormal results.

Low Vaccination Coverage

Health officials emphasize that being vaccinated against HPV is the best protection for preventing cervical cancer in women, as well as several other types of cancer in women and men. According to a study published in January 2013, nationally only 32 percent of girls aged thirteen to seventeen had received the recommended three doses as of 2010. Shown on this map is a state-by-state breakdown of nationwide HPV vaccine coverage.

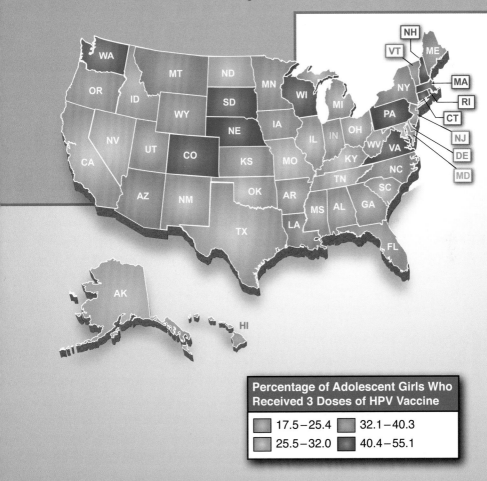

Percentage of Adolescent Girls Who Received 3 Doses of HPV Vaccine

17.5–25.4	32.1–40.3
25.5–32.0	40.4–55.1

Source: Ahmedin Jemal et al., "Annual Report to the Nation on the Status of Cancer, 1975–2009, Featuring the Burden and Trends in Human Papillomavirus (HPV) – Associated Cancers and HPV Vaccination Coverage Levels," *Journal of the National Cancer Institute*, January 2013. http://jnci.oxfordjournals.org.

Should the HPV Vaccine Be Mandatory?

66The types of HPV, human papillomavirus, that commonly cause cervical cancer in women has dropped by about half in girls aged 14 to 19 since 2006 when we began routinely vaccinating against HPV.99

—Thomas R. Frieden, director of the CDC.

66This aspect of mandatory vaccination is a political hot button. State mandates override parental consent, fueling long-standing antivaccination movements.99

—Lawrence O. Gostin, an attorney with the O'Neill Institute for National and Global Health Law who specializes in public health law.

In January 2013 health officials released a comprehensive report on the status of cancer in the United States. It was the culmination of a collaborative effort that involved researchers from the American Cancer Society, National Cancer Institute, CDC, and North American Association of Central Cancer Registries. A positive message came through on the report: A downward trend that began more than a decade ago is continuing, with death rates for all cancers combined decreasing among both men and women. But that good news was accompanied by a revelation that was anything but positive. Some cancers, including HPV-associated cancers of the anus and oropharynx, were on the rise. The team also found that nationwide, only 32 percent of girls aged thirteen to seventeen had received the recommended three doses of the HPV vaccine. In the published report, the authors conclude: "Increases in incidence rates for some HPV-associated cancers and low vaccination coverage among adolescents underscore the need for additional prevention efforts for HPV-associated cancers, including efforts to increase vaccination coverage."[56]

When the study findings were announced, medical groups, physicians, and infectious disease experts were quick to express their opinions. One who spoke out was Dr. Harold Varmus, director of the National Cancer Institute, who stated during an interview that the report "correctly and usefully emphasizes the importance of HPV infection as a cause of the growing number of cancers of the mouth and throat, the anus, and the vulva, as well as cancers of the uterine cervix, and the availability of vaccines against the major cancer-causing strains of HPV." Varmus went on to predict that that there would be problems in the future if action was not taken to reverse the trend. "The investments we have made in HPV research to establish these relationships and to develop effective and safe vaccines against HPV will have the expected payoffs only if vaccination rates for girls and boys improve markedly."[57]

> When the study findings were announced, medical groups, physicians, and infectious disease experts were quick to express their opinions.

Why Parents Say No

Varmus's concerns are shared by other health officials and physicians who emphasize that the HPV vaccine saves lives. They want to know why vaccination rates are so low and what can be done to raise them. One study whose purpose was to closely examine this issue was led by Oklahoma pediatrician Paul M. Darden. For the study, which was published in April 2013, the researchers analyzed a long-term CDC survey of American families with thirteen- to seventeen-year-old children. This was a comprehensive survey in which parents were asked a number of general questions about vaccinations, including the HPV vaccine. If they had chosen not to vaccinate a child, the parents were asked to share their reasons for that decision. The study authors write: "The objective for this project was to determine the reasons parents choose not to vaccine their adolescents with specific vaccines and how these reasons have changed over time."[58]

Darden's team found that a disturbing number of parents admitted to having no plans to have their daughters vaccinated against HPV. In 2008, among those parents whose daughters were not up-to-date on the HPV vaccine, 40 percent said they had no intention of having the girls get it. By 2010 that number had risen to 44 percent of parents. "Despite doctors increasingly recommending adolescent vaccines," the authors write, "parents increasingly intend not to vaccinate female teens with HPV."[59] When parents were asked why they made this decision, the primary reasons given were frequently vague. For example, slightly more than 17 percent said it was "not necessary," and others said "lack of knowledge" and "don't know."[60]

> "A disturbing number of parents admitted to having no plans to have their daughters vaccinated against HPV.

Another finding of the study illustrated how misinformed many people are about the HPV vaccine. Slightly more than 11 percent of parents said their daughters did not need the vaccine because they were not sexually active. That is an erroneous perception, because the HPV vaccine is designed to be given before young people are sexually active, largely because contracting the virus is so common. After young people become infected with HPV (and most will never know if they are), the vaccine cannot do anything to protect them against the strain of the HPV they have contracted.

Lives Saved

Despite the disappointing vaccination rate and the negative attitudes of many parents toward the vaccines, the CDC reported some surprisingly good news in June 2013. Researchers led by CDC physician and preventive medicine expert Lauri E. Markowitz studied prevalence of HPV infection from 2003 to 2010. The group analyzed a comprehensive national survey in which health workers interviewed more than eight thousand girls and women aged fourteen to fifty-nine, from whom vaginal swabs were collected and analyzed by the CDC. Markowitz's team found that within four years of Gardasil's introduction, prevalence of HPV types 6, 11, 16, and 18 had decreased from 11.5 percent in 2003 to 5.1 percent in 2010—a decline of 56 percent. According to Markowitz, there are several possible reasons for prevalence to drop even though vaccination rates were low. One possibility is a phenomenon known as herd immunity, in which vaccinated individuals reduce the overall prevalence of the virus in society. This in turn decreases the chances that un-vaccinated people will be exposed to someone who is infected.

> " In the United States decisions about issues such as mandating a particular vaccine are typically left up to the states rather than the federal government. "

When the study findings were announced, CDC director Thomas R. Frieden did not hesitate to express how pleased he was to hear about them and also what needed to happen to keep the momentum going. "These are striking results," says Frieden. "They should be a wake-up call that we need to increase vaccination rates. The bottom line is this: It is possible to protect the next generation from cancer, and we need to do it."[61]

State Actions

In the United States decisions about issues such as mandating a particular vaccine are typically left up to the states rather than the federal government. The debate over the HPV vaccine issue first began to emerge in 2006. After Gardasil became available, the CDC's Advisory Committee on Immunization Practices (ACIP) announced that routine vaccination was recommended for young girls. The National Conference of State Legislatures (NCSL) writes: "Even after recommendations by the ACIP, school vaccination requirements are decided mostly by state legislatures."[62]

The NCSL adds that among the states, a major focus of the debate has been school vaccine requirements, which have always been determined by state law. "Some people who support availability of the vaccine do not support a school mandate," says the NCSL, "citing concerns about the drug's cost, safety, and parents' rights to refuse. Still others may have moral objections related to a vaccine mandate for a sexually transmitted disease. . . . This has caused some to push for further discussion and debate about whether or not to require the vaccine."[63]

> **The HPV vaccine debate is complicated as well as contentious, which is why so few state legislatures have succeeded in getting laws passed.**

According to the NCSL, at least forty-two US states and territories have introduced some type of legislation related to the HPV vaccine. Michigan and Ohio both tried and failed to mandate the vaccine in 2006. The following year Texas became the first state to succeed at mandating the vaccine—and the issue was hotly debated. Governor Rick Perry boldly bypassed the state legislature and issued an executive order that mandated the HPV vaccine for all girls who were entering the sixth grade. Opponents of the vaccine denounced Perry's actions, and he addressed his critics in a February 5, 2007, statement:

> Never before have we had an opportunity to prevent cancer with a simple vaccine. While I understand the concerns expressed by some, I stand firmly on the side of protecting life. . . . In the past, young women who have abstained from sex until marriage have contracted HPV from their husbands and faced the difficult task of defeating cervical cancer. This vaccine prevents that from happening. Providing the HPV vaccine doesn't promote sexual promiscuity anymore than providing the Hepatitis B vaccine promotes drug use. If the medical community developed a vaccine for lung cancer, would the same critics oppose it claiming it would encourage smoking?[64]

Perry's executive order did not stand, and he lost the fight for the vaccine mandate. In May 2007 the Texas legislature passed a law that overturned his order and barred mandatory HPV vaccinations until the year 2011. Rather than vetoing the bill, Perry opted to let it become law without his signature.

As of April 2014 only Virginia and Washington, DC, had legislation in place that made the HPV vaccine mandatory. Virginia's law, which was passed in October 2008, requires that girls have all three of the recommended vaccine doses, with the first completed before the start of the sixth grade. Parents may elect for their child not to receive the vaccine, but only after reviewing materials provided by the state board of health. Since Virginia passed its HPV vaccine legislation, there have been several attempts to repeal it, but none has been successful.

Parents' Rights

The HPV vaccine debate is complicated as well as contentious, which is why so few state legislatures have succeeded in getting laws passed. One of the strongest and most passionate objections is that the vaccination of a child should be the parents' decision, rather than being mandated by the government. Denise J. Hunnell, a physician and retired US Air Force major from Virginia, acknowledges that there are many aspects to the mandatory vaccine debate. She is convinced, though, that the "real root" of the controversy is not the vaccine itself but rather "who gets to make the decision to vaccinate: the government or parents."[65]

Hunnell has followed the vaccine debate closely and is aware of the various viewpoints. She says the fear that young people would "run wild once they were protected" from HPV has been debunked; there is no evidence that the vaccine leads to "increased promiscuity" as some have alleged. Another concern, that the vaccine is not safe, has also proved to be unfounded, as she explains: "Both Gardasil and Cervarix . . . appear to be mostly safe. A recent review of nearly 200,000 girls who received the HPV vaccine showed no statistically significant ill effects."[66] Hunnell's concern is that any effort to make the vaccine mandatory infringes on parental rights to make health-care decisions for their children. She writes:

> The bottom line is that both the decision to vaccinate and the decision not to vaccinate against HPV are reasonable choices. Parents have the right to weigh the risks and benefits of the HPV vaccine and make a decision based on their own unique situations. The state has offered no

convincing argument to justify usurping parental rights and mandating HPV vaccines. To do so attacks the integrity of the family and benefits the corporate interests of [the pharmaceutical companies] far more than it benefits the health of American men and women.[67]

Determining how parents feel about an HPV vaccine mandate was the focus of a study by researchers from the University of Michigan CS Mott Children's Hospital. In January 2012 they polled more than two thousand adults and asked a number of questions about adolescent health care. When asked whether they would support state laws that allow teens to receive the HPV vaccination without parental consent, only 45 percent said they would. When those who did not support forgoing parental consent were asked their reasons, 43 percent cited side effects of the vaccine and 40 percent voiced moral and/or ethical concerns. But by far the most common reason—cited by 86 percent of participants—was that whether to vaccinate should be a parent's decision.

The Debate Rages On

Mandating the HPV vaccine is as contentious as any public issue ever has been. Despite strong recommendations from the CDC and other agencies that all youth be vaccinated, many parents still choose not to abide by that—and this is true even though studies have shown that the vaccine is curbing the prevalence of HPV infection. Even many who are in favor of the vaccine are against the government telling parents what they must do with their own children. Because of the nature of this debate and the strong opinions on all sides, it will likely not be resolved anytime in the near future.

Should the HPV Vaccine Be Mandatory?

" The rapidly growing body of research . . . can allow the whole community including doctors, medical researchers, parents and other interest groups to be more confident that the benefits of HPV vaccination far outweigh the risks."

—David Hawkes, Candice E. Lea, and Matthew J. Berryman, "Answering Human Papillomavirus Vaccine Concerns; a Matter of Science and Time," Infectious Agents and Cancer, June 12, 2013. www.infectagentscancer.com.

Hawkes, Lea, and Berryman are researchers from Australia.

" Nothing has convinced me that the benefits of the HPV vaccine outweigh the risks—which are significant."

—Christiane Northrup, "The HPV Vaccine: What You Need to Know Today," *Dr. Northrup's Blog*, August 1, 2013. www.drnorthrup.com.

Northrup is an obstetrician/gynecologist who focuses on women's health and wellness.

Primary Source Quotes

66 **The HPV vaccine is a significant public health milestone, and we, as a field, need to work at correcting misconceptions about the vaccine and work with governments to pass HPV vaccine mandates for all boys and girls.** 99

—Tanya Donahou, "HPV Vaccine Controversy: Ethics, Economics, and Equality," *Movement* (Boston University School of Public Health), Spring 2012. www.bu.edu.

At the time this paper was published, Donahou was an MD/MPH candidate at the Boston University School of Medicine and Public Health.

66 **Despite doctors increasingly recommending adolescent vaccines, parents increasingly intend not to vaccinate female teens with HPV.** 99

—Paul M. Darden et al., "Reasons for Not Vaccinating Adolescents: National Immunization Survey of Teens, 2008–2010," *Pediatrics*, March 12, 2013. http://pediatrics.aappublications.org.

Darden is a pediatrician from Oklahoma City, Oklahoma.

66 **Declines in genital warts cases have been reported in countries that have implemented national vaccination programs.** 99

—Allison Friedman, Charles Ebel, and Raymond Maw, "Counseling the Patient with Genital HPV Infection," in *Sexually Transmitted Infections: Diagnosis, Management, and Treatment*, eds. Jonathan M. Zenilman and Mohsen Shawmanesh. Sudbury, MA: Jones & Bartlett, 2012, p. 301.

Friedman is a health community specialist with the CDC, Ebel is a researcher from North Carolina, and Maw is a physician from Belfast, Northern Ireland.

66 **The CDC has investigated many of the deaths allegedly attributed to the [HPV] vaccine and found that there's no consistent pattern, and nothing that links them to getting the immunization.** 99

—Aaron E. Carroll, "The HPV Vaccine and Why Your Kids Should Get It," video, Healthcare Triage, November 17, 2013. www.youtube.com.

Carroll is a professor of pediatrics and assistant dean for research mentoring at Indiana University School of Medicine.

66HPV vaccination has the potential to reduce cervical cancer deaths around the world by as much as two-thirds, and to prevent anal cancer in males and females.99

—National Cancer Institute, "Human Papillomavirus (HPV) Vaccines," December 29, 2011. www.cancer.gov.

The National Cancer Institute is the federal government's principal agency for cancer research and training.

66Vaccine coverage is hindered by public perceptions regarding HPV's status as a sexually transmitted infection and dissent over the recommended age of vaccination. Social conservatives have countered vaccine mandates with the argument that they infringe upon parental rights to discuss the topic of sex on their own terms.99

—Karlie A. Intlekofer et al., "The HPV Vaccine Controversy," *Virtual Mentor*, January 2012. http://virtualmentor.ama-assn.org.

Intlekofer is a postdoctoral fellow at the Institute for Memory Impairments and Neurological Disorders at the University of California–Irvine.

66We should step aside and allow young men and women—and their parents—the freedom to decide if getting the HPV vaccine is a wise investment in their future health.99

—Michele Promaulayko, "The Vilification of a Vaccine," *Huffington Post*, October 6, 2011. www.huffingtonpost.com.

Promaulayko is vice president and editor in chief of *Women's Health* magazine.

Facts and Illustrations

Should the HPV Vaccine Be Mandatory?

- According to the NCSL, in 2006 the Michigan senate was the first to introduce legislation to **require the HPV vaccine** for girls entering sixth grade, but the bill was not enacted.

- The NCSL reports that as of November 2013 twenty-five states and territories had enacted some type of **HPV vaccination policy**, but only Virginia and Washington, DC, had mandated the vaccinations.

- A June 2013 fact sheet by the Kaiser Family Foundation states that access to HPV vaccines is **limited** mostly to affluent populations in developed countries.

- In a Quinnipiac University poll released in February 2012, more than **half** of Virginia voters said they wanted the state law requiring girls to be vaccinated against HPV to be repealed.

- In a study of multicultural parents published in December 2010, nearly all participants expressed support for making HPV vaccinations **mandatory**.

- In June 2013 Japan's Ministry of Health issued a statement that it had formally withdrawn its recommendation for adolescent girls to receive the HPV vaccination due to reports of **severe side effects**.

- According to a study published in the June 2013 issue of the *Journal of Infectious Diseases*, the prevalence of HPV infections among American adolescent girls markedly declined after the HPV vaccine became available in 2006, falling **56 percent** by 2010.

Poll: Parental Consent Should Be Required

One common objection to the HPV vaccination becoming mandatory is that it usurps parents' rights to make health-care decisions for their children. To gauge public support for such a mandate, reseachers from the University of Michigan conducted a survey in 2012 that involved 2,131 adults. When asked whether state laws should allow HPV vaccinations without parental consent, most did not favor such legislation.

Public support for state laws allowing adolescents age 12–17 to receive medical care without parental consent.

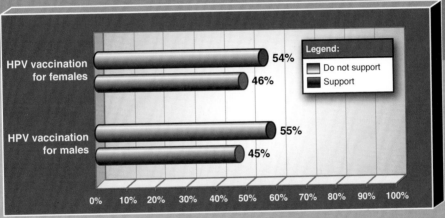

Source: University of Michigan C.S. Mott Children's Hospital, "National Poll on Children's Health," July 18, 2012. www.mottnpch.org.

- According to the CDC, the primary benefits of **vaccinating males** against HPV include protection against genital warts, anal cancer, and transmission of HPV to sexual partners.

- The National Cancer Institute reports that both HPV vaccines have been tested on tens of thousands of people in the United States and other countries, and **no serious side effects** have been directly linked to either vaccine.

Objection to Mandate

From 2007 to 2010 researchers from Harvard University School of Public Health conducted a study to examine state HPV vaccination policies throughout the United States. Shown here are some factors that were identified as impeding the passage of laws similar to those that require immunization for measles, tetanus, whooping cough, etc., before a child starts school.

Object to HPV Vaccine Mandate Because...	Explanation
Newness of the vaccine	Long-term safety data needed before a vaccine mandate could be justified.
The sexually transmitted nature of HPV	Could potentially send the wrong message to young people about having sex; also, requiring a girl to be vaccinated at age eleven or twelve could force parents to have discussions about sex before they are ready to do so.
Not a contagious disease	Unlike communicable diseases such as chicken pox, for which vaccines prevent the spread in schools, HPV is not contagious through casual contact in the classroom.
Discomfort with the vaccine manufacturer's involvement in policy making	Many respondents viewed Merck's lobbying for the vaccine as questionable and possibly inappropriate.
The price of the vaccine	Concern that some families could not afford to have their children vaccinated and also that the cost would consume too much of states' shares of Medicaid and public health budgets.
Opposition to government coercion	Objections to government mandates in general.
Anti-vaccination activism	Some organizations and individuals were convinced that vaccines cause autism and other health problems in children.

Source: Robert Wood Johnson Foundation, "How Laws Have Encouraged Use of a New Vaccine by Preteen Girls," *Program Results Report*, October 14, 2013. www.rwjf.org.

Why Parents Choose Not to Vaccinate

Overall HPV vaccination coverage is low in the United States, and this is disturbing to health officials. To better understand parents' reasons for not vaccinating their children, University of Oklahoma researcher Paul M. Darden and his colleagues published a study in 2013. The main reasons given are shown on this graph.

Main reasons given for parent(s) choosing not to vaccinate

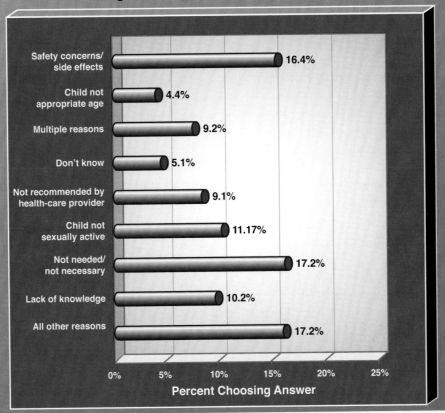

Source: Paul M. Darden et.al., "Reasons for Not Vaccinating Adolescents: National Immunization Survey of Teens, 2008–2010," *Pediatrics*, March 18, 2013. http://pediatrics.aappublications.org.

- A 2012 study by researchers at the University of Texas Southwestern Medical Center found that black females aged twelve to seventeen were **35 percent** less likely than white females to receive a health-care provider recommendation for the HPV vaccine.

Key People and Advocacy Groups

American Sexually Transmitted Diseases Association: A leading advocacy organization that is dedicated to the control and study of STDs.

Centers for Disease Control and Prevention (CDC): As the United States' leading health protection agency, the CDC is charged with promoting health and quality of life by controlling disease, injury, and disability.

Food and Drug Administration: A federal organization charged with keeping products safe and effective, monitoring products for continued safety once they are in use, and providing the public with accurate, science-based information.

Ian Hector Frazer: An Australian scientist whose extensive research led to the development of the first vaccine to guard against high-risk HPV types.

Maura Gillison: A noted scientist and HPV expert who was the first to implicate HPV infection as a leading cause of oral cancer.

Immunization Action Coalition: A group that works to increase immunization rates and prevent disease by educating health professionals and the public.

National Cervical Cancer Coalition: An organization that is dedicated to serving women who have or are at risk for cervical cancer and other types of HPV-related disease.

National Institute of Allergy and Infectious Diseases: An agency of the National Institutes of Health that conducts and supports research to better understand, treat, and ultimately prevent infectious, immunologic, and allergic diseases.

George N. Papanicolaou: A scientist who is known for his cancer research and invention of the Pap smear, a diagnostic test for cervical cancer detection.

Planned Parenthood Federation of America: An organization that provides health-care services, sex education, and sexual health information to women, men, and young people through its nearly nine hundred health centers throughout the United States.

Keerti Shah: A virologist who in 1999 announced that 99.7 percent of cervical cancer cases are caused by HPV infection.

Richard E. Shope: An American scientist who was the first to isolate the papillomavirus in cottontail rabbits and observe that the virus induced warts.

Elizabeth Stern: A Canadian pathologist who was the first to link a specific virus (herpes simplex) to a particular cancer (cervical cancer). Although her identification of the virus was incorrect, Stern has been lauded for research that led to better diagnostic tests for early detection and treatment of cervical cancer.

Harald zur Hausen: A German virologist who was the first to prove that HPV causes cervical cancer.

Chronology

1999
Based on investigations of HPV prevalence among women from twenty-two countries, Johns Hopkins virologist Keerti Shah and his colleagues announce that HPV accounts for more than 99 percent of cervical cancer cases.

1898
Dutch scientist Martinus Willem Beijerinck is the first to use the word *virus* to describe infectious organisms that are even smaller than bacteria.

1928
Greek scientist George N. Papanicolaou presents a paper that introduces the idea of using vaginal smears to detect uterine cancer in cells. Although his concept is not well received, the Pap test eventually becomes the leading method of detecting cervical cancer in women.

1970
British scientists J.D. Oriel and June D. Almeida announce that they have discovered virus particles in human genital warts, although they cannot determine whether there is a relationship between these and common skin warts.

1900

1970

2000

1907
During experiments on himself, Italian physician Giuseppe Ciuffo confirms the infectious nature of human warts.

1974
At an international conference in Florida, German virologist Harald zur Hausen angers attendees by publicly refuting the prevailing scientific belief that cervical cancer is caused by the herpes simplex virus; he suggests that the focus instead should be on papillomaviruses.

1983
Hausen and colleagues publish a paper stating that they have isolated HPV types 16 and 18, thus proving the existence of multiple HPV strains.

1931
German scientists Ernst Ruska and Max Knoll invent the electron microscope, which makes it possible to view organisms such as viruses that are too small to be seen with ordinary microscopes.

1933
In experiments with cottontail rabbits, American scientist Richard E. Shope becomes the first to isolate the papillomavirus, and he discovers that it induces warts.

2001
After clinical trials, the HPV vaccine Gardasil is determined to be effective in protecting against HPV types 6, 11, 16, and 18.

2011
At a news conference, CDC officials announce that HPV vaccination rates are lagging far behind other vaccines that are specifically recommended for teens and preteens.

2010
The CDC announces that Gardasil is recommended for males aged nine through twenty-six for the prevention of genital warts and some types of HPV-associated cancer.

2013
A study by a team of researchers from Sweden leads to the discovery of twenty-three new strains of HPV.

2006
The FDA announces its approval of the vaccine Gardasil for females aged nine to twenty-six.

2000

2010

2003
The FDA approves the use of HPV DNA testing, in combination with the Pap test, to screen women older than thirty for cervical cancer.

2012
A study published in the *Journal of the American Medical Association* reveals that an estimated 7 percent of American teens and adults carry HPV in their mouths, which researchers say proves that oral sex plays a role in transmission of the virus.

2007
Texas governor Rick Perry issues an executive order requiring that girls entering the sixth grade be vaccinated for HPV; the Texas legislature passes a bill to override the executive order, and Perry does not veto it.

2009
The FDA approves the release of a second HPV vaccine, Cervarix, which helps prevent cervical cancer and precancerous lesions caused by HPV types 16 and 18.

2014
A study by researchers from Sweden reveals that women previously treated for abnormal cells on the cervix have an increased risk of dying from cervical or vaginal cancer compared with the general female population, and the risk increases after age sixty.

Related Organizations

American Cancer Society

National Headquarters
250 Williams St.
Atlanta, GA 30303
phone: (404) 320-3333; toll-free: (800) 227-2345
website: www.cancer.org

The American Cancer Society is a nationwide, community-based, voluntary health organization that is dedicated to eliminating cancer as a major health problem. Its website search engine produces a number of articles about HPV and its association with cancer.

American College of Obstetricians and Gynecologists (ACOG)

409 Twelfth St. SW
PO Box 70620
Washington, DC 20024-9998
phone: (202) 638-5577; toll-free: (800) 673-8444
website: www.acog.org

With approximately fifty-five thousand physician members, ACOG serves as an advocate for quality health care for women. Its website provides a number of articles and fact sheets about HPV and other STDs.

American Sexual Health Association

PO Box 13827
Research Triangle Park, NC 27709
phone: (919) 361-8400 • fax: (919) 361-8425
e-mail: info@ashastd.org
website: www.ashastd.org

The American Sexual Health Association serves as a source of reliable information on sexual health. Its website offers a great deal of information about HPV and other STDs, including news releases, fact sheets, and reports, along with a link to the organization's blog.

Centers for Disease Control and Prevention (CDC)

1600 Clifton Rd.
Atlanta, GA 30333
phone: (404) 498-1515; toll-free: (800) 311-3435 • fax: (800) 553-6323
e-mail: inquiry@cdc.gov
website: www.cdc.gov

As the United States' leading health protection agency, the CDC is charged with promoting health and quality of life by controlling disease, injury, and disability. Its STD website features a special section on HPV with numerous informative publications.

Immunization Action Coalition

1573 Selby Ave., Suite 234
St. Paul, MN 55104
phone: (651) 647-9009 • fax: (651) 647-9131
e-mail: admin@immunize.org
website: www.immunize.org

The Immunization Action Coalition works to increase immunization rates and to prevent disease by educating health professionals and the public. A wide variety of materials about HPV are available through its website, and a search engine produces numerous articles about vaccinations and other HPV-related topics.

Mayo Clinic

200 First St. SW
Rochester, MN 55905
phone: (507) 284-2511 • fax: (507) 284-0161
website: www.mayoclinic.com

The Mayo Clinic is a world-renowned medical practice that is dedicated to the diagnosis and treatment of virtually every type of complex illness and disease. Its website search engine produces a number of publications about HPV-related topics.

National Cancer Institute (NCI)

NCI Office of Communications and Education
Public Inquiries Office
6116 Executive Blvd., Suite 300
Bethesda, MD 20892-8322
phone: (301) 496-1038; toll-free: (800) 422-6237
e-mail: cancergovstaff@mail.nih.gov
website: www.cancer.gov

An agency of the National Institutes of Health, the NCI is the principal federal agency for cancer research and training. A wide variety of publications on HPV-related topics are available through the website's search engine.

National Cervical Cancer Coalition (NCCC)

6520 Platt Ave., #693
West Hills, CA 91307
phone: (818) 909-3849; toll-free: (800) 685-5531 • fax: (818) 780-8199
e-mail: info@nccc-online.org
website: www.nccc-online.org

The NCCC is dedicated to serving women who have or are at risk for cervical cancer and other types of HPV-related disease. Its website offers health articles available through a searchable database, cervical cancer and HPV topics, survivor stories, and a quarterly *Extraordinary Moments* newsletter.

National Institute of Allergy and Infectious Diseases (NIAID)

Office of Communications and Government Relations
6610 Rockledge Dr., MSC 6612
Bethesda, MD 20892-6612
phone: (301) 496-5717; toll-free: (866) 284-4107 • fax: (301) 402-3573
e-mail: ocpostoffice@niaid.nih.gov
website: www.niaid.nih.gov

An agency of the National Institutes of Health, the NIAID conducts and supports research to better understand, treat, and ultimately prevent infectious, immunologic, and allergic diseases. A variety of informative publications about HPV are available by using the site's search engine.

Planned Parenthood Federation of America

434 W. Thirty-Third St.
New York, NY 10001
phone: (212) 541-7800; toll free: (800) 230-7526 • fax: (212) 245-1845
website: www.plannedparenthood.org

Through its network of affiliates that operate nearly nine hundred health centers, Planned Parenthood provides health-care services, sex education, and sexual health information to women, men, and young people. The search engine on its website produces numerous articles about HPV-related topics.

For Further Research

Books

Jennifer Bringle, *Young Women and the HPV Vaccine*. New York: Rosen, 2011.

Nicholas Collins and Samuel G. Woods, *Frequently Asked Questions About STDs*. New York: Rosen, 2011.

Roman Espejo, ed., *Sexually Transmitted Diseases*. Detroit, MI: Greenhaven, 2011.

Brandie Gowey, *Your Cervix Just Has a Cold*. Garden City, NY: Morgan James, 2014.

H. Hunter Handsfield, *Color Atlas and Synopsis of Sexually Transmitted Diseases*. New York: McGraw- Hill, 2011.

Jacqueline Langwith, ed., *HPV*. Detroit: Greenhaven, 2013.

Lawrence R. Stanberry and Susan L. Rosenthal, *Sexually Transmitted Diseases: Vaccines, Prevention, and Control*. London: Academic Press, 2013.

Periodicals

Sarah Brown, "Calling the Shots," *Vogue*, December 2011.

Melissa Bykotky, "The 411 on HPV," *Marie Claire*, November 2013.

Stephanie Findlay, "An Ounce of Prevention," *Maclean's*, January 21, 2013.

Denise Grady, "Troubles with Heart Are Linked to HPV," *New York Times*, October 24, 2011.

James Hamblin, "The Cancer Vaccine," *Atlantic*, November 2013.

Rachel Heller, "Most. Awkward. Second. Date. Ever.," *Marie Claire*, November 2013.

Jazelle Hunt, "HPV Vaccines Less Effective for Black Women," *Charlotte (NC) Post*, November 19, 2013.

Shobha S. Krishnan, "The HPV Vaccine Controversy," *Skeptical Inquirer*, January–February 2012.

Monte Morin, "HPV Vaccination Rate Stalls. 'We're Dropping the Ball,' CDC Says," *Los Angeles Times*, July 25, 2013.

Patt Morrison, "Surprise—HPV Vaccine Doesn't Make Good Girls Go Bad," *Los Angeles Times*, October 16, 2012.

Anahad O'Connor, "Throat Cancer Link to Oral Sex Gains Notice," *New York Times*, June 3, 2013.

Genevra Pittman, "Despite Evidence, Parents' Fears of HPV Vaccine Grow," *Chicago Tribune*, March 18, 2013.

Nathan Seppa, "Dose of Reality: HPV Is Epidemic, Which Is Odd Since It Is Largely Preventable," *Science News*, April 20, 2013.

Sabrina Tavernise, "HPV Vaccine Is Credited in Fall of Teenagers' Infection Rate," *New York Times*, June 19, 2013.

Laura Vozzella, "Why the Politics of HPV Are So Muddled," *Washington Post*, September 17, 2011.

Rachel Walden, "What You Need to Know About the HPV Vaccine," *Women's Health Activist*, July–August 2013.

Internet Sources

Brooke Carey, "HPV and Cervical Cancer: What My Boyfriend and I Didn't Know," *The Blog, Huffington Post*, January 21, 2013. www.huffingtonpost.com/brooke-carey/hpv-cervical-cancer-boyfriend-and-i-didnt-know_b_2444775.html.

Centers for Disease Control and Prevention, "Genital HPV Information—Fact Sheet," March 2013. www.cdc.gov/std/hpv/HPV-Fact-sheet-March-2013.pdf.

Kate-Madonna Hindes, "20 Million Mind-Blowing Statistics About HPV and Cancer," *Minnesota Blog Cabin*, MinnPost, June 26, 2012. www.minnpost.com/minnesota-blog-cabin/2012/06/20-million-mind-blowing-statistics-about-hpv-and-cancer.

Megan McCardle, "Why You Should Vaccinate Your Sons for HPV," Daily Beast, June 3, 2013. www.thedailybeast.com/articles/2013/06/03/why-you-should-vaccinate-your-sons-for-hpv.html.

Rachel Rettner, "Can You Give HPV to Yourself?," Live Science, November 11, 2013. www.livescience.com/41090-oral-hpv-self-inoculation.html.

ScienceDaily, "HPV Vaccination Rates Alarmingly Low Among Young Women in Southern US," October 30, 2013. www.sciencedaily.com/releases/2013/10/131030132854.htm.

Megan Scudellari, "HPV: Sex, Cancer and a Virus," *Nature*, November 20, 2013. www.nature.com/news/hpv-sex-cancer-and-a-virus-1.14194.

Alexandra Sifferlin, "HPV Vaccine Doesn't Lead to Promiscuous Tweens," *Time*, August 15, 2012. http://healthland.time.com/2012/10/15/hpv-vaccine-doesnt-lead-to-promiscuous-tweens.

WebMD, "Information About the Human Papillomavirus," February 16, 2012. www.webmd.com/sexual-conditions/hpv-genital-warts/hpv-virus-information-about-human-papillomavirus.

Source Notes

Overview

1. Anonymous, "I Caught an STI the First Time I Had Sex," Everyday Feminism, October 4, 2012. http://everydayfeminism.com.
2. Anonymous, "I Caught an STI the First Time I Had Sex."
3. Anonymous, "I Caught an STI the First Time I Had Sex."
4. American Cancer Society, "Human Papilloma Virus (HPV), Cancer, HPV Testing, and HPV Vaccines: Frequently Asked Questions," October 22, 2013. www.cancer.org.
5. American Cancer Society, "Human Papilloma Virus (HPV), Cancer, HPV Testing, and HPV Vaccines."
6. Throat Cancer Foundation, "Why Is HPV a Problem?," January 8, 2013. www.throat cancerfoundation.org.
7. Centers for Disease Control and Prevention, "Genital HPV Infection—Fact Sheet," July 24, 2013. www.cdc.gov.
8. Valerie R. Yanofsky, Rita V. Patel, and Gary Goldenberg, "Genital Warts: A Comprehensive Review," *Journal of Clinical Aesthetic Dermatology*, June 2012. www.ncbi.nlm.nih.gov.
9. Robin Wallace, "The Common Cold of the Sexually Active World," Bedsider, 2011. http://bedsider.org.
10. Quoted in Meredith Holt, "HPV Facts: While Most People Carry HPV, Most Will Never Know It," Inforum, June 8, 2012. www.inforum.com.
11. Marie Savard, "Human Papillomavirus, HPV," Healthy Women, April 4, 2013. www.healthywomen.org.
12. Margaret J. Meeker, "Risky Business: An Interview with Dr. Meg Meeker," Life Athletes, January 2006. www.lifeathletes.org.
13. World Health Organization, "Human Papillomavirus (HPV) and Cervical Cancer," September 2013. www.who.int.
14. American Cancer Society, "Finding Cervical Pre-Cancers," May 2, 2013. www.cancer.org.
15. WebMD, "HPV Infection in Men," HPV/Genital Warts Health Center, February 16, 2012. www.webmd.com.
16. Jason D. Wright, "Patient Information: Management of a Cervical Biopsy with Precancerous Cells (Beyond the Basics)," UpToDate, August 4, 2013. www.uptodate.com.
17. Quoted in Denise Grady, "A Vital Discussion, Clouded," *New York Times*, March 6, 2007. www.nytimes.com.
18. National Cervical Cancer Coalition, "Myths and Facts," 2013. www.nccc-online.org.
19. Quoted in Richard Knox, "HPV Vaccine: The Science Behind the Controversy," National Public Radio, September 19, 2011. www.npr.org.
20. Quoted in Rachel Rettner, "Should the HPV Vaccine Be Mandatory? Health Experts Weigh In," Live Science, September 14, 2011. www.livescience.com.
21. Quoted in Rettner, "Should the HPV Vaccine Be Mandatory? Health Experts Weigh In."

What Is HPV?

22. Harald zur Hausen, interviewed by Adam Smith, "Interview," NobelPrize.org, October 6, 2008. www.nobelprize.org/nobel_prizes/medicine/laureates/2008/hausen-tele phone.html.

23. Quoted in Stephen Pincock, "Virologist Wins Nobel for Cervical Cancer Discovery," *Lancet*, October 18, 2008. http://download.thelancet.com.

24. American Cancer Society, "Human Papilloma Virus (HPV), Cancer, HPV Testing, and HPV Vaccines."

25. Throat Cancer Foundation, "Why Is HPV a Problem?"

26. Wallace, "The Common Cold of the Sexually Active World."

27. Lina Michala et al., "Human Papilloma Virus Infection in Sexually Active Adolescent Girls," *Gynecologic Oncology*, August 2012. www.ncbi.nlm.nih.gov.

28. Lea E. Widdice et al., "Prevalence of Human Papillomavirus Infection in Young Women Receiving the First Quadrivalent Vaccine Dose," *Archives of Pediatric Adolescent Medicine*, August 2012. http://archpedi.jamanetwork.com.

29. Renata Mírian Nunes Eleutério et al., "Prevalence of HPV in Adolescents Virgins and Sexually Active at a University Hospital in the City of Rio de Janeiro, Brazil," *ISRN Infectious Diseases*, June 2013. www.hindawi.com.

30. National Cervical Cancer Coalition, "Myths and Facts."

31. Megan Trad, Robert F. Reardon, and Dominic Caraveo, "Understanding HPV and the Future Implications of Contracting the Virus," *Radiologic Technology*, May/June 2013. www.radiologictechnology.org.

What Are the Health Risks of HPV?

32. Quoted in Mary Shedden, "Cancer Survivor Advocating for Men's HPV Awareness," *Tampa Bay Tribune*, July 28, 2013. http://tbo.com.

33. Quoted in Irene Maher, "Fighting and Surviving Oral Cancer," *Tampa Bay Times*, September 8, 2010. www.tampabay.com.

34. Quoted in Shedden, "Cancer Survivor Advocating for Men's HPV Awareness."

35. American Cancer Society, "Oral Cavity and Oropharyngeal Cancer," June 18, 2013. www.cancer.org.

36. Quoted in Megan Scudellari, "HPV: Sex, Cancer and a Virus," *Nature*, November 20, 2013. www.nature.com.

37. Quoted in Scudellari, "HPV."

38. Quoted in Scudellari, "HPV."

39. Quoted in Alexandra Sifferlin, "How Brushing Your Teeth Lowers Your Risk of Cancer," *Time*, August 21, 2013. http://healthland.time.com.

40. Quoted in Scudellari, "HPV."

41. Mary M. Gallenberg, "Disease and Conditions," Mayo Clinic, July 9, 2011. www.mayo clinic.org.

42. Kate-Madonna Hindes, "Cervical Cancer Does Not Define Me," *Minnesota Business Magazine*, June 2012. www.womenspress.com.

43. Hindes, "Cervical Cancer Does Not Define Me."

44. J.G. Palmer et al., "Anal Cancer and Human Papillomavirus," *Diseases of the Colon & Rectum*, December 1989. http://link.springer.com.

45. American Society of Colon & Rectal Surgeons, "Anal Cancer," October 2012. www .fascrs.org.

46. Quoted in Laura Perry, "HIV Plus HPV Leads to Increased Anal Cancer Risk in Men," *UCLA Newsroom*, December 2, 2013. http://newsroom.ucla.edu.

47. Quoted in ScienceDaily, "Some Lung Cancers Linked to Common Virus," April 10, 2013. www.sciencedaily.com.

Can HPV Infection Be Prevented?

48. Otis Webb Brawley, "No More Annual Pap Smear: New Cervical Cancer Screening Guidelines," *CNN Health*, March 15, 2012. www.cnn.com.

49. Quoted in Jonathan R. Cole, *The Great American University*. New York: Public Affairs, 2009, p. 222.

50. Paul A. Elgert and Gary W. Gill, "George N. Papanicolaou, MD, PhD," *Lab Medicine*, April 2009. http://labmed.ascpjournals.org.

51. National Cancer Institute, "Human Papillomavirus (HPV) Vaccines," December 29, 2011. www.cancer.gov.

52. Bryce Covert, "I Had HPV and Lived to Tell the Tale," *Feministing* (blog), September 16, 2011. http://feministing.com.

53. Ricki Pollycove, "Condoms Not Effective Against HPV or Herpes," *San Francisco Chronicle*, January 21, 2013. www.sfgate.com.

54. Thanh Cong Bui et al., "Examining the Association Between Oral Health and Oral HPV Infection," *Cancer Prevention Research*, August 2013. www.ada.org.

55. Quoted in Sifferlin, "How Brushing Your Teeth Lowers Your Risk of Cancer."

Should the HPV Vaccine Be Mandatory?

56. Ahmedin Jemal et al., "Annual Report to the Nation on the Status of Cancer, 1975–2009, Featuring the Burden and Trends in Human Papillomavirus (HPV)–Associated Cancers and HPV Vaccination Coverage Levels," *Journal of the National Cancer Institute*, January 2013. http://jnci.oxfordjournals.org.

57. Harold Varmus, "Report to the Nation Shows U.S. Cancer Death Rates Continue to Drop; Special Feature Highlights Trends in HPV-Associated Cancers and HPV Vaccination Coverage Levels," news release, National Cancer Institute, January 7, 2013. www.cancer.gov.

58. Paul M. Darden et al., "Reasons for Not Vaccinating Adolescents: National Immunization Survey of Teens, 2008–2010," *Pediatrics*, March 18, 2013. http://pediatrics.aap publications.org.

59. Darden et al., "Reasons for Not Vaccinating Adolescents."

60. Quoted in Darden et al., "Reasons for Not Vaccinating Adolescents."

61. Quoted in Sabrina Tavernise, "HPV Vaccine Is Credited in Fall of Teenagers' Infection Rate," *New York Times*, June 19, 2013. www.nytimes.com.

62. National Conference of State Legislatures, "HPV Vaccine," January 2014. www.ncsl.org.

63. National Conference of State Legislatures, "HPV Vaccine."

64. Quoted in Office of the Governor Rick Perry, "Statement of Gov. Rick Perry on HPV Vaccine Executive Order," news release, February 5, 2007. http://governor.state.tx.us.

65. Denise J. Hunnell, "HPV Vaccine Controversy Is About Rights and Transparency, Not Sex and Health," *CNS News*, October 19, 2012. http://cnsnews.com.

66. Hunnell, "HPV Vaccine Controversy Is About Rights and Transparency, Not Sex and Health."

67. Hunnell, "HPV Vaccine Controversy Is About Rights and Transparency, Not Sex and Health."

List of Illustrations

Index

About the Author

Peggy J. Parks holds a bachelor of science degree from Aquinas College in Grand Rapids, Michigan, where she graduated magna cum laude. An author who has written more than one hundred educational books for children and young adults, Parks lives in Muskegon, Michigan, a town that she says inspires her writing because of its location on the shores of Lake Michigan.